TABLE OF CONTENTS

HOW TO USE THIS BOOK

RIGHT Answers: The Answers to 260 of Your Retirement Questions provides you with 260 questions about issues relating to retirement and retirement income with the answers to those questions.

We have written this book as if you were asking us the questions: what you might ask, and how we would answer. For this reason, there is some information overlap between some questions. However, we have tried to keep this to a minimum while still ensuring that all answers have enough detail to be accurate.

We put this book and its q&a concept to a focus group of people nearing retirement or already retired and every one fully supported our approach, especially the use of "everyday language" to make answers easy to understand.

We're always ready to hear more of your questions. Please send them and comments to info@rightseminars.com.
Sam Albanese
Susan Yates

ITABMA?
(IS THERE ANOTHER BUSINESS WITH MORE ACRONYMS?)

Here are some acronyms you may hear in discussions about retirement. Not all are expanded upon in the following text. Each entry lists:

- the **acronym**;
- what it stands for;
- *the broad subject matter the entry relates to*;
- a brief definition.

A&S
Accident and Sickness Insurance
health insurance
A broad category of insurance that includes critical illness, accidental death, disability, health, travel, dental, vision, prescription drug, and long-term care insurance.

ACB
Adjusted cost base
investment
The cost of acquiring capital property, such as an investment, minus its value when sold.

ACB
Adjusted cost basis
life insurance
The cost of making an investment in an insurance policy minus the gain from disposing of part or all of the policy.

CDIC
Canada Deposit Insurance Corporation
banking
A Crown Corporation that insurers against the insolvency of banks and similar financial institutions to specified limits.

CFP
Certified Financial Planner
designation
An international designation attained upon completion of a course of study about personal financial matters. In Canada, the designation is administered by the Financial Planning Standards Council (FPSC).

CII
Critical Illness Insurance
health insurance
A form of insurance that pays out its face value when the insured becomes ill with one of the conditions covered by the policy and survives 30 days post-diagnosis.

CIPF
Canadian Investor Protection Fund
investment
An organization that protects members of the public who invest through investment dealers against insolvency of the dealers to specified limits.

CLU
Chartered Life Underwriter
designation
A designation attained by those who complete the course of studies about life and health insurance, and successfully complete the exam(s).

CPB
Canada Premium Bond
investment
A bond issued by the Government of Canada that offers a slightly better interest rate than a Canada Savings Bond, and can be cashed in at any time.

CPP
Canada Pension Plan
government pensions
The retirement savings plan to which all Canadians who work contribute after age 18, providing they earn more than the minimum threshold amount.

CRA
Canada Revenue Agency
taxation
The agency of the federal government that collects tax from individuals, businesses, and charities.

CSB
Canada Savings Bond
investment
A bond issued by the Government of Canada with a guaranteed interest rate. A CSB can be cashed at any time. They are now only available through payroll savings plans.

CSC
Canadian Securities Course
investment
The course that must be completed by anyone who wishes to become a stockbroker in Canada. Cannot be advertised by those who have completed the program.

CSV
Cash Surrender Value
life insurance
The amount received in cash by a life insurance policy owner who sacrifices his or her whole life or universal life policy.

DBP
Defined Benefit Plan
company pensions
A pension with a pre-determined guaranteed payment.

DCP
Defined Contribution Plan
company pensions
A pension that is not guaranteed and whose amount is a result of investment choices made by the employee.

DPSP
Deferred Profit Sharing Plan
company pensions
A registered retirement plan that provides a pension to employees. Only the employer contributes to the plan. Payment is received as either cash, company stock, payments over a 10-year period, or a life annuity.

ETFs
Exchange Traded Funds
investment

ETFs are an investment product in which investors own shares in a fund that represent all the components of a chosen index (e.g., the TSX) or multiple indexes. The shares are bought and sold through a stock exchange.

FV
Future Value
money management
The value of an investment at a future date, which is the sum of principal plus returns.

GIC
Guaranteed Investment Certificate
investment
An investment product that, for the most part, guarantees return of principal plus interest after the specified period of investment
(e.g., three years).

GIS
Guaranteed Income Supplement
government pension
A retirement pension available to low-income seniors who receive OAS.

GLWB
Guaranteed Lifetime Withdrawal Benefit Plans
investment
The same as GMWB except the payout period is for life.

GMWB
Guaranteed Minimum Withdrawal Benefit Plan
investment
An investment product sold by life insurers that offers a guaranteed income with the potential for capital appreciation.

The investor has the option to defer withdrawals and receive a credit for every year they do not make a withdrawal. Payouts are made over a specified number of years as the higher of either a minimum guaranteed amount or the market value of the segregated fund in which the principal is invested.

GRSP
Group Retirement Savings Plan
company pensions
Like an individual RRSP, except the employer that offers the plan administers accounts on a group basis. Employers match employee contributions. GRSPs are not locked in.

HBP
Home Buyers Plan
RRSPs
A plan that permits those with RRSP accounts to access their savings in order to make a downpayment on a qualified home.

HELOC
Home Equity Line of Credit
real estate
A line of credit available on an as-needed basis to a home owner. The amount is determined as a percentage of equity in the home.

IIROC
Investment Industry Regulatory Organization of Canada
investing
The Canadian association of stockbrokers and investment dealers that regulates its members and ensures their compliance with securities laws.

IPC
Investor Protection Corporation
investing
The organization that acts as an insurer of investor accounts to specified limits if a member of the Mutual Fund Dealer's Association becomes insolvent.

IVIC
Individual Variable Investment Contract
life insurance
This is the full name for a segregated fund or seg fund. A seg fund is an investment provided by life insurance companies similar to a mutual fund but with guaranteed returns and a ten-year term-to-maturity.

JTWROS
Joint Tenancy With Rights of Survivorship
legal
A form of property ownership in which there are two joint "tenants" or owners. When one joint tenant dies, the surviving joint tenant becomes the owner of the property. This is a means of bypassing probate on the co-owned property.

LIF
Life Income Fund
company pensions
An account that can accept a rollover of funds from a LIRA and from which withdrawals can be made. It is not available in PEI.

LIRA
Locked-in Retirement Account
company pensions
An account to which the value of a registered pension plan can be transferred to continue tax deferral. Such an account

is an intermediary step between the administration of the pension by the employer and the "eventual" account that permits withdrawals to be made. Eventual accounts include a Life Income Fund, Prescribed Retirement Income Fund (PRIF) or Locked-in Retirement Income Fund (LRIF).

LLP
Lifelong Learning Plan
RRSPs
A plan that permits those with RRSPs to access those savings to use for adult education.

LLQP
Life License Qualification Program
insurance
The training program that must be completed by those who wish to sell life insurance or accident and sickness insurance. Cannot be advertised by those who have completed the program.

LRIF
Locked-in Retirement Income Fund
company pensions
Similar to a LIF except there is no requirement to convert plan value to an annuity at any time. They are available in AB, MB, ON and NL.

LTC OR LTCI
Long-Term Care Insurance
health insurance
Insurance to pay the cost of care when the insured is unable to perform certain activities or has cognitive impairment.

MER
Management Expense Ratio
investing
An annual cost stated as a percentage that is charged
to mutual fund investors for management by the fund
management company.

MFDA
Mutual Fund Dealer's Association
investing
The association of mutual fund dealers that regulates
its members.

MTR
Marginal Tax Rate
taxation
Basically, the rate at which an individual pays income tax.

NAV
Net Asset Value
investing
The price per unit of a mutual fund determined as the total
value of holdings minus liabilities divided by number of
units outstanding.

OAS
Old Age Security
government pensions
The retirement pension paid to all Canadians who meet
residency requirements.

PRB
Post-Retirement Benefit
government pensions
The contribution made to the Canada Pension Plan by
someone who has already started taking a CPP pension

but who returns to work or continues to work. The PRB is mandatory between 60 and 65, and optional between 65 and 70.

PRIF
Prescribed Retirement Income Fund
company pensions
Only available to members of registered pension plans in Saskatchewan and Manitoba. The account continues the tax deferral of locked-in funds; there is a minimum withdrawal but no maximum.

PRPP
Pooled Registered Pension Plan
company pensions
A new form of company pension that will be introduced when legislation is finalized. PRPPs are designed for smaller companies and the self-employed. Contributions are pooled so that plan members will benefit from the lower investment management costs associated with the scale of these funds.

PV
Present Value
money management
An amount in today's dollars that will equal a specified sum in the future. It is a result of the principal plus returns between today and the future date.

QPP
Quebec Pension Plan
government pensions
The equivalent plan to CPP as provided in Quebec.

RDSP
Registered Disability Savings Plan
savings
A savings account that permits tax-free growth on contributions. Proceeds of the account are earmarked for the use of a disabled Canadian child or adult.

RLIF
Restricted Life Income Fund
federal pensions
A tax-deferred savings account for those with a federal pension. It is similar to a LIF but must be used when a person is employed by one of the industries in which pensions are federally regulated, such as banking.

RPP
Registered Pension Plan
company pensions
The broad category that includes all forms of company pension plans such as defined benefit plans (DBPs) and defined contribution plans (DCPs).

RRIF
Registered Retirement Income Fund
savings
A retirement savings account to which an RRSP can be transferred. Tax is deferred until money is withdrawn and then it is taxed as income. A minimum withdrawal must be made based on age.

RRSP
Registered Retirement Savings Plan
savings
A retirement savings account to which contributions are tax deductible but withdrawals are taxed as income. Tax is deferred until money is withdrawn.

SWR
Safe Withdrawal Rate
investing
An amount that can be withdrawn annually from
retirement savings that will ensure savings are never
depleted because investment growth compensates for
withdrawals.

T-100
Term-to-100
life insurance
A form of life insurance that terminates at death or age 100
(whichever event comes first). It offers the lowest premium
cost relative to coverage than either whole life insurance or
universal life insurance.

TEP
Trust and Estate Practitioner
designation
An international designation bestowed by the Society of
Trust and Estate Practitioners (STEP).

TFSA
Tax-free Savings Account
taxation
A savings account in which contributions are not tax
deductible but withdrawals are tax free.

UL
Universal Life Insurance
life insurance
A form of permanent life insurance with an investment
component.

YMPE

Year's Maximum Pensionable Earnings
Canada Pension Plan
This is the maximum amount of earnings, set annually, on which contributions to CPP are calculated.

401K

401K

company pension plans (US)
A company pension plan to which employees in the US contribute; employers may contribute also. Earnings in the plan are tax deferred.

GENERAL CONCERNS

This chapter introduces some general questions; in some cases more detail is provided in other chapters and you will be directed there accordingly. This chapter is unique in that it addresses the single biggest concerns to those contemplating retirement or already retired: how much do I need to save, and how do I make the money last. Also, see question 13 if your retirement includes living outside Canada.

QUESTIONS:

1. How much do I need to save to retire?
   How much do we need to save?
2. How can I increase my retirement income?
3. What age should I retire at?
4. Will I get OAS and CPP automatically on retirement?
5. When should I convert my RRSP to a RRIF?
6. Will I get my company pension automatically when I retire?
7. What if I retire and then decide to go back to work? Do I lose my pensions?
8. Can I make retirement income simple and easy?
9. How do I make sure my money lasts as long as I do?

10. Are there any income or pension benefits couples can look forward to that aren't available if you're single?
11. How long should I plan for?
12. Do I need a will?
13. I'm considering retiring and moving to Costa Rica. Are there special considerations if I move out of Canada?
14. What are the biggest risks facing retirees?

HERE ARE THE ANSWERS...

1:   How much do I need to save to retire? How much do we need to save?

You will hear a lot of numbers thrown around for how much retirement will cost. One of the common ones is 70% of pre-retirement household income. In other words, if you earn $80,000 per year when you are working, you will need $56,000 per year when you are retired. If you and your spouse earned $125,000, then together you'd need $87,500.

If you multiplied the sum for a single person ($56,000) by 30, for 30 years of retirement, and did not take inflation or investment returns into account, you would calculate that you would need $1.68 million saved when you retire. Most individuals are not going to be able to save even close to such a large amount, and they become extremely discouraged when they hear numbers such as this. Even when you take the value of OAS and CPP pensions into consideration, which can contribute hundreds of thousands to the pot over the 30-year period, most will still find themselves woefully short of savings.

There are many problems with taking an approach like 70% of income: most notably, who is to say that 70% is too much or too little? It depends very much on your personal circumstances for expenses.

A better way to answer this question is to estimate how much you think you would realistically spend on a monthly basis when you are retired.

Start by making a list of your current monthly bills for:

- your mortgage, rent, or condo fee;

- property taxes;

- transportation costs and car insurance;

- heat, hydro, water, phones, cell phones & internet, cable TV;

- groceries;

- eating out;

- shopping;

- medical costs for prescription drugs or other expenses;

- insurance premiums for life / disability / mortgage insurance and travel / health insurance;

- minimum payments for credit cards, line of credit, loans, etc.;

- any other costs you have, which could include memberships, entertainment, etc.;

- miscellaneous costs for gifts, salon services, etc.

Total these costs for your household, whether you are single or a couple. This estimate gives you a very rough cut on your minimum costs. It does not take into consideration, for instance, how much it will cost to replace your car every so often, or to replace or repair large items around your home, such as if you needed a new furnace or new roof. However, let's just set those expenses aside to see whether your basic living expenses can be covered by your retirement income.

Next, consider what these monthly costs might be when you are retired and put those numbers beside the others on your list. Some expenses may go down when you don't have to go to work every day, but some expenses may go up. To keep it simple, use costs as they would be today. Don't try and guess how much inflation would increase these costs. Again, total the costs. Now, just out of interest, you know whether they are 70% of pre-retirement income or not.

Do you have enough retirement income to pay your anticipated living costs? Find out by adding together your sources of income --- government pensions like we have already mentioned, a pension you might get from your employer, plus any income from a business or rental property.

For your RRSP savings, use 4% of its value divided by 12 to show its monthly contribution to income. For instance, if you have $150,000 in your RRSP, that amount equates to $500/month income ($150,000 multiplied by 4% divided by 12). The reason 4% is used for withdrawals is that 4% is considered a "safe withdrawal rate" for invested savings that would not deplete the savings before age 90. (You will actually find you are required to take more than 4% from your RRSP/RRIF after age 65, but let's just use 4% to give you a minimum number to use in this exercise.)

There's one big "but." You must subtract an amount for income tax from that calculation of income. Since we can't know what future income tax rates might be, play this conservatively and use the percentage of tax you currently pay. Now you have a net income number.

When you subtract your proposed expenses from your net retirement income you'll have a much better idea of whether your income, based on your pensions and savings, is going to be enough to live on, rather than simply assuming you need 70% of salary.

If you have more income than you need, then you have money available for the lump-sum expenses we described above plus, if you're lucky, the fun side of retirement whatever that means for you: travel, putting your grandkids through university, buying a second home, or giving to charity.

If you have less income than your expenses, you must increase income, delay your retirement date, or cut expenses.

2: How can I increase my retirement income?

You can:

- Work longer or get a job during retirement – the job could be seasonal, part-time or on contract.

- Pay off your debts while you are still working so your need for income is less.

- Sell assets, such as your home, and use the proceeds to create an income stream. This is called asset harvesting.

- Delay starting both your OAS and CPP pensions to increase their monthly value.

- Take more than the minimum RRIF withdrawal. However, your RRIF account will be depleted faster when you take more than the minimum and you risk running out of money.

Seek tax advantages available to you including: splitting income, keeping non-registered funds in a Tax-Free Savings Account (TFSA), and investing non-registered savings in investments that pay dividends or capital gains. Both forms of return are taxed at lower rates than interest bearing investments.

3:   What age should I retire at?

There is no age at which you must retire in Canada. Therefore, you can pick your retirement age according to what suits you best. If you want to retire and you can afford to retire, do it!

Full CPP pension benefits are not paid until age 65. OAS can begin at age 65 or later. Both pensions pay more per month when you wait after age 65 to start receiving them.

Your private pension from your employer may also specify the age for "normal" retirement but this does not mean you must retire at that age.

4:   Will I get OAS and CPP automatically on retirement?

No. You must apply. See the following chapter on government pensions.

5: When should I convert my RRSP to a RRIF?

Make the conversion to a RRIF when you are certain you
will no longer want to make any more RRSP contributions
and/or when you want to start taking money out.
Once the RRSP is converted to a RRIF you must begin
withdrawing the annual minimum from the account
regardless of your age.

You can, of course, make a withdrawal from your RRSP
whenever you want but there will be a withholding
tax based on how much you withdraw, and where you
live since a different rate applies in Quebec. There is no
withholding tax on minimum RRIF withdrawals.

You can also have an RRSP and a RRIF at the same time
until the end of the year when you turn 71. Then your
RRSPs must be converted to one of the maturity options
that are available. A RRIF is one of the options.

See the following chapter on RRSPs and RRIFs.

6: Will I get my company pension automatically when
     I retire?

If you are enrolled in a defined benefit plan, your pension
will begin whenever you specify and according to the
limitations of the plan. For instance, the pension may
specify that payments cannot begin before age 60.
You will receive the amount of pension promised in your
pension statement.

If you are enrolled in a defined contribution plan, your
pension statement will not promise a certain amount that
you will receive when you retire. On retirement, you must

transfer the funds in the plan to a locked-in retirement account (LIRA), LIF (Life Income Fund), PRIF (Prescribed Retirement Income Fund), or annuity. The annuity will pay a specified amount. Withdrawals are not permitted from the LIRA; it is a holding account only. To get money out, you will have to transfer from the LIRA to the LIF/PRIF; the amount you receive will depend on how much you transfer, how you invest the value of the account, and the minimum and maximum withdrawal allowed. See the following chapter on company pensions.

7: What if I retire and then decide to go back to work? Do I lose my pensions?

Once your pensions begin you will not stop receiving them until you die; some pensions will continue to pay your spouse after your death. The exception to this is that if your income exceeds the level at which Old Age Security is cut off, and then you would lose your OAS pension until your income level dropped. Then your OAS would be reinstated.

If you return to work between age 60 and 65 and you had started CPP, you will have to contribute to the CPP Post-Retirement Benefit (PRB) at the same rate as your CPP contributions were made. In other words, it is as if you are contributing to CPP while you are receiving CPP. If you work past age 65, contributing to the PRB is not mandatory.

8: Can I make retirement income simple and easy?

Yes. Retirement income planning and strategies are designed to maximize the amount of money coming in and minimize what you pay in tax. For this reason, they try to balance many variables to arrive at a best plan of action. This can be a complicated endeavour.

However, income during retirement does not have to be complicated. It can be made very simple by:

- applying for OAS and CPP at retirement and receiving the pensions every month by direct deposit to your bank account;

- converting your savings, RRSP, or LIRA (Locked-in Retirement Account) to an annuity and receiving the money every month;

- receiving any other income owing to you;

- paying tax on the amount you receive.

9:   How do I make sure my money lasts as long as I do?

Everything you do to reduce debt while you are still employed --- so that you need less money when you are retired --- is going to help your money last.

When debt is reduced, you will be able to:

- take the minimum amount each year from your RRIF or other plan if you have a company pension, such as a Life Income Fund (LIF);

- stick to the so-called safe withdrawal rate for your non-registered investment accounts. This rate should not be more than 4% per year of the value of the accounts.

In addition, you may be able to reduce expenses associated with later life if you take out a long-term care insurance policy. This policy will ensure that you do not need to fund long-term care costs from your own pocket.

Also, you can look to annuities as a guaranteed source of income that can be depended on for life. They aren't glamourous but you'll always know your annuity income will be there as long as you need it.

Other life insurance products also provide an income for life. Please see the life insurance chapter for details.

10: Are there any income or pension benefits couples can look forward to that aren't available if you're single?

In the following pages we will present many ideas that apply to spouses. To briefly summarize: Spouses enjoy definite economic advantages that aren't available to those who are single or do not have a legal or common-law spouse.

1. A couple is able to base their RRIF withdrawals on the age of the younger spouse. This will mean less money must be taken out from the plan as an annual minimum so the money in the plan will last longer.

2. A couple who has different marginal tax rates can split income from a RRIF, or pension once they qualify for the pension tax credit at age 65. Splitting income moves income from one spouse who pays tax at a higher marginal tax rate to the other, who pays at a lower rate. This will save on income tax.

3. A couple can enjoy the benefit of a spousal RRSP. Spousal RRSPs were of greater use before pension income splitting was introduced a few years ago. In a spousal RRSP one spouse contributes to the RRSP of the other --- again to take advantage of different tax rates. Since income splitting was introduced, a spousal RRSP continues to be useful if one spouse is older than 71 and the other is younger. The older spouse can contribute to the younger spouse's plan.

4. A couple can also choose to "assign" their CPP pension. This splits both pensions in half and assigns each half to each person. This will also have tax benefits if there is a discrepancy in the marginal tax rates of the two.

5. An RRSP and a RRIF can rollover to a spouse tax-free if the plan owner dies.

6. A registered pension plan is the type of pension received from an employer. The spouse of a registered pension plan member must receive at least 60% of the plan member's pension if he or she dies. The only way to avoid this obligation is for the spouse of the plan member to sign a waiver indicating he or she agrees to forgo the pension if his or her spouse dies.

The real benefit to couples is the two incomes they earn during their working lives, the two sets of pensions they may receive from employers and CPP, and their lower cost of living per person which enables them to save more. Single people must pay all living costs entirely from their own pocket, which leaves many economically disadvantaged in retirement compared to those who are married.

11:   How long should I plan for?

The most difficult question of all! You can refer to actuarial tables to predict your lifespan. However, they are averages and what if you aren't average? What if you are one of the 50% who live longer than the average?

Your alternative to playing the game of averages is to look at your family health history and ages at death. Factor in your own lifestyle factors that could contribute to your life being longer or shorter than others in your family. Remember, married people live longer on average than those who are single.

There are many reasons to plan for longevity instead of underestimating. No one wants to consider what kind of life they would have to live if they ran out of money and had to rely solely on government pensions.

And, if you died sooner than you planned, undoubtedly someone would be pleased to receive an unexpected or unexpectedly larger bequest.

12:   Do I need a will?

Yes. Every person with any form of asset and/or family responsibilities (spouse and/or children) needs to have a will. It will make things easier for your survivors, and can save them time and money in dealing with your estate. Remind your children, too, that they should have wills — and make sure they know where yours is stored.

13: I'm considering retiring and moving to Costa Rica. Are there special considerations if I move out of Canada?

Yes. Residential ties to Canada will be broken if:

- your home is no longer in Canada;

- your spouse or dependants are no longer in Canada;

- you do not have personal property, such as a car, in Canada;

- you no longer have social or economic ties to Canada.

Your Canadian residency may also be severed if you:

- no longer have accounts at Canadian financial institutions;

- don't have a driver's license issued by a Canadian jurisdiction;

- no longer are entitled to provincial health insurance.

When you are no longer a Canadian resident you will become a non-resident for tax purposes. As long as you are a non-resident you must complete a tax return if you earn income from Canadian sources.

Some of these income sources include:
- pension payments;
- OAS;

- CPP/QPP;
- RRSP payments;
- RRIF payments;
- annuity payments.

In the year you leave you report on your tax return:

- your world income that you received while you were still a Canadian resident;

- your Canadian-only income earned when you were no longer a Canadian resident.

RRSPs/RRIFs

If you are a non-resident and decide to cash out your RRSP, you will pay a withholding tax of 25% on your withdrawal. The country in which you live may also want to tax the withdrawal.

If the country has an income tax treaty with Canada, the withholding tax on periodic payments for withdrawals from a RRIF may be set at 15%, if certain conditions are met.

Employer Pensions

Locked-in pension funds, such as those deposited to a Life Income Fund (LIF) or locked-in RRSP, can be unlocked if the plan owner is no longer a Canadian resident. Once the funds are unlocked they can be transferred to a regular bank or investment account. Tax will be applied to withdrawals.

CPP

Your CPP benefit can be paid to you anywhere in the world.

OAS

You will receive OAS outside Canada if you lived in Canada for at least 20 years after turning 18, or you lived or worked in a country that has a social security agreement with Canada and your application is approved.

TFSA

If you emigrate from Canada and have a TFSA, you can keep your TFSA and continue to benefit from tax-free withdrawals. However, no further contributions will be allowed and no contribution room will accrue while you are a non-resident.

Tax expertise should be obtained if you are considering becoming a Canadian non-resident retiree.

14:   What are the biggest risks facing retirees?

There are three significant risks particular to retirement.

1. Longevity risk in which lifespan exceeds funding. In other words, your money runs out before you do. This risk is addressed by saving more, working longer, spending less, or some combination of these.

2. Investment risk in which returns do not compensate for withdrawals, investment losses, and inflation. To combat this risk retirees need to find best returns for guaranteed investments.

3. Cognitive risk in which the effects of aging impair decision-making and poor financial decisions result. Some experts believe this can start as young as age 55. This risk can be mitigated by ensuring

a power of attorney for property is in place and can make necessary financial decisions when you can no longer reliably make such decisions for yourself. Another solution is the creation of an *inter vivos* trust; assets are placed in the trust and administered by a trustee while you are alive.

GOVERNMENT-PROVIDED PENSIONS

Here are the details on all forms of federal government pensions and additional income benefits available provincially.

GENERAL

15. Are government pensions important to retirement income planning?
16. Do all Canadians get OAS and CPP?
17. How often are CPP and OAS paid?
18. How can I find out how much I'm going to get in CPP and OAS pension payments?
19. Are CPP and OAS payments taxable income?
20. Will I receive the same amount as a pension for life from CPP and OAS?
21. Do I have to be legally married to receive spousal benefits?
22. Do I receive the same benefits if I am in a same sex relationship?

CANADA PENSION PLAN

23. What is CPP?
24. When should I start CPP?

25. How much more will I get in my CPP by waiting after I'm 65 to start?

26. How much will I lose if I start my CPP before age 65?

27. I think I will live to age 92. Am I better to start the CPP early when it is going to be a lower amount but I will receive it for more years, or wait until I'm older and get more as a pension but for fewer years?

28. Will I receive CPP? When, and how do I get it?

29. How is the amount of my CPP pension determined?

30. Will I receive CPP automatically?

31. How do I apply for CPP?

32. What is the Post-Retirement Benefit?

33. I contributed to CPP for life. If I die, would my spouse receive any money from my CPP?

34. When do payments begin for the survivor's pension?

35. Can I receive CPP while I continue to work?

36. Will I receive my CPP pension if I leave Canada?

37. Do same sex partners receive spousal benefits?

38. Does CPP provide a payment on death?

39. My spouse and I split up. Can I get some of those CPP contributions as a pension?

40. Are there any tax reduction strategies to use with CPP?

41. If I continue to work after 60, even though I receive the CPP, do I still make CPP contributions?

42. What are the factors that will contribute to how much I will get in CPP?

43. I stayed at home to raise my children. Will that affect my CPP?

Old Age Security

Guaranteed Income Supplement (GIS)

The Allowance

VETERAN'S BENEFITS

65. Is a pension available for war veterans?
66. How do I apply?

PROVINCIAL/TERRITORIAL BENEFITS

67. I live in Alberta.
    Are any other income benefit programs available for me?
68. I live in BC. Are any other income benefit programs available for me?
69. I live in Manitoba. Are any other income benefit programs available for me?
70. I live in Saskatchewan. Are any other income benefit programs available for me?
71. I live in Ontario. Are any other income benefit programs available for me?
72. I live in Quebec. Are any other income benefit programs available for me?
73. I live in Nova Scotia. Are any other income benefit programs available for me?
74. I live in New Brunswick. Are any other income benefit programs available for me?
75. I live in Prince Edward Island. Are any other income benefit programs available for me?
76. I live in Newfoundland and Labrador. Are any other income benefit programs available for me?
77. I live in the Yukon. Are any other income benefit programs available for me?
78. I live in Nunavut. Are any other income benefit programs available for me?
79. I live in Northwest Territories. Are any other income benefit programs available for me?

HERE ARE THE ANSWERS...

15: Are government pensions important to retirement income planning?

Absolutely yes! Government pensions contribute a significant amount of income over time: you would have to save hundreds of thousands more if you did not qualify to receive them. Furthermore, they are permanent and they are guaranteed.

16: Do all Canadians get OAS and CPP?

All Canadians who meet the residency requirements for living in Canada get OAS. Only those who have paid into the plan through employment receive CPP, or if a person is the surviving spouse of someone who made CPP contributions, It is also possible for a separated or divorced spouse of a CPP contributor to receive some of that contributor's CPP.

17: How often are CPP and OAS paid?

Both pensions are paid monthly. They can be paid by cheque or direct deposit to your bank account.

18: How can I find out how much I'm going to get in CPP and OAS pension payments?

The government provides two helpful tools to help you calculate what you are going to receive during retirement:

one is the Benefits Finder that will give you a personalized list of benefits that you may be entitled to receive. It can be accessed at:

**http://www.canadabenefits.gc.ca/
f.1.2cw.3zardq.5esti.4ns@.jsp**

The other is the Canadian Retirement Income Calculator that will provide an estimate of both OAS and CPP benefits. The Calculator is available at:

**http://www.servicecanada.gc.ca/
eng/isp/common/cricinfo.shtml**

It takes about 30 minutes to complete the details for the Calculator. For the greatest degree of accuracy when using the Calculator you need to be prepared with:

- CPP Statement of Contributions or QPP Statement of Participation;

- information about your employer pension (if you have one);

- recent RRSP statement(s);

- statements for other savings that will provide ongoing monthly retirement income (annuities, foreign pensions; survivor pensions, etc.).

19: Are CPP and OAS payments taxable income?

Yes. You must declare the amount you have received as pension income in the year on your income tax return for that year.

20: Will I receive the same amount as a pension for life from CPP and OAS?

Once they begin, their benefits are fixed for life except both CPP and OAS pay different rates and each is indexed for inflation. CPP is adjusted every January. OAS pensions are reviewed in January, April, July and October to reflect increases in the cost of living as measured by the Consumer Price Index. The increases keep the pensions in line with inflation.

If your income reaches specified limits, your OAS pension may be reduced or eliminated. It can be reinstated in part or full if income falls.

21: Do I have to be legally married to receive spousal benefits?

No. Common-law partners have the same benefits as legally married spouses.

22: Do I receive the same benefits if I am in a same sex relationship?

You will receive the same benefits whether you are common-law partners or legally married.

23: What is CPP?

CPP is the Canada Pension Plan (note that this should not be confused with the insurance company that calls itself CPP which stands for Canada Protection Plan). It provides a retirement pension to all Canadians who have worked, made a valid contribution to the plan, and are at least 60 years old.

If you were a CPP contributor, your spouse can receive a portion of your pension if you die. This is called a survivor's benefit. It is available to a legally married or common-law spouse.

In Quebec, the plan is called the Quebec Pension Plan or QPP. It provides the same monetary benefits as CPP to those who live in Quebec or work for a Quebec employer.

24: When should I start CPP?

You can begin receiving CPP at age 60. At one time you needed to prove you had little or no income for two consecutive months before you could receive CPP. That is no longer true. There is no need to prove you need the money to start receiving the CPP; you simply apply.

However, if you do not need the money from the CPP, the longer you wait the higher the amount of each pension cheque will be up to the maximum entitlement at age 70. From age 70 on, you will not receive more by waiting; you do receive adjustments according to increases in the cost of living.

The amount you receive whenever you begin CPP will be what you receive for life, except that the pension amount is adjusted to keep pace with inflation.

25: How much more will I get in my CPP by waiting until after I'm 65 to start?

Starting in 2013, you will receive 0.7% per month or 8.4% per year more by waiting. This increase is applied every month until age 70 when there are no further increases due to waiting.

26: How much will I lose if I start my CPP before age 65?

The amount of reduction pre-age 65 is a gradual decrease as follows:

- in 2013, minus 0.52% per month (6.24% per year)
- in 2014, minus 0.56% per month (6.72% per year)
- in 2015, minus 0.58% per month (6.96% per year)
- in 2016 and thereafter, minus 0.6% per month (7.2% per year)

27: I think I will live to age 92. Am I better to start the CPP early when it is going to be a lower amount but I will receive it for more years, or wait until I'm older and get more as a pension but for fewer years?

It is estimated that by 2016, the annual CPP pension will be about $4,000 less at age 60 than if it was started at age 65 and about $4,600 more if it was delayed from age 65 to age 70.

At age 90, the person who began CPP at age 70 will collect about $100,000 more in total pension payments than the retiree who began at age 60. Therefore, lifespan has a bearing: if you believe you will live a longer life, and can afford to wait, then wait to get more --- a lot more as it turns out.

28:   Will I receive CPP? When, and how do I get it?

You can receive CPP at age 60 if you apply, have worked, and have made a valid contribution to the plan. CPP is paid monthly. The amount is adjusted every January if there has been an increase in the cost of living as measured by the Consumer Price Index. This way, the pension keeps pace with inflation. If the cost of living goes down, the pension does not follow suit.

29:   How is the amount of my CPP pension determined?

The amount you will receive as a CPP pension is a result of contributions made into the plan, the limits set by the federal government for the pension, and the age at which you choose to begin your pension.

Contributions are made when you earn more than the minimum threshold the government sets. You will also find that 7.5 years (for 2013, 8 years in 2014) of lowest earnings are not taken into account.

If you choose to begin CPP before 65, you are penalized for every month you receive the pension before that age. If you choose to begin CPP later than 65, you will receive a bonus in the form of an increase to your pension for every month you wait. Whether you are penalized, receive a bonus because you wait, or receive the standard-age 65 pension, that amount is what you receive for life except for the ongoing adjustments for inflation.

30:   Will I receive CPP automatically?

No. You must apply to receive the pension and it is suggested that you apply at least six months ahead of time.

31:   How do I apply for CPP?

You can apply online at:
**http://www.servicecanada.gc.ca/eng/isp/common/
rtrinfo.shtml**

Or, you can print out the form from this site, complete it,
and mail it in:
**http://www.servicecanada.gc.ca/eforms/forms/
sc-isp-1000(2012-05-18)e.pdf**

32:   What is the Post-Retirement Benefit?

The Post-Retirement Benefit (PRB) was implemented in
2012. It applies to you if you are between 60 and 70 if you
receive CPP and continue to work. Contributions to the
PRB must be made if you are between 60 and 64; they
are optional if you are between 65 and 70. The payment
supplements the CPP pension and provides a small
additional income for life. No further contributions can be
made after age 70.

33:   I contributed to CPP for life. If I die, would my
spouse receive any money from my CPP?

A survivor's pension is paid monthly to the surviving
spouse of a deceased CPP contributor. You may qualify if
you are separated from your deceased spouse and he or
she does not have a cohabiting common-law partner.

There are three factors that determine how much your
surviving spouse will receive as a survivor's pension:

1. his or her age when you die;

2. how much you contributed to the plan and for how long;

3. whether your spouse is already receiving a CPP pension.

34: When do payments begin for the survivor's pension?

A survivor's pension is paid monthly to the surviving spouse of a deceased CPP contributor. The survivor must apply to receive the pension; processing takes between six and 12 weeks. However, the pension will be paid as if it started the month after the contributor's death so several back payments may be included when the pension is first received. CPP can make back payments for up to 12 months.

35: Can I receive CPP while I continue to work?

Yes. You will be required to pay into the Post-Retirement Benefit Plan until you turn 65; thereafter contributions are optional up to age 70. This plan supplements your income starting the year after you begin contributions.

36: Will I receive my CPP pension if I leave Canada?

Yes. Payments may be made in the currency of the country in which you reside; for instance, in the US your pension will be paid in US dollars.

37: Do same sex partners receive spousal benefits?

Yes.

38: Does CPP provide a payment on death?

Yes: up to $2,500 will be paid to the estate of the deceased contributor. If there is no estate, the person responsible for the funeral expenses, the surviving spouse or common-law partner, or the next of kin may be eligible, in that order.

39: My spouse and I split up. Can I get some of those CPP contributions as a pension?

CPP credits accrue while a couple lives together and at least one of them pays into the plan. If the relationship ends, the credits can be divided equally between them. This is called credit splitting and applies whether both spouses paid into the plan or only one paid.

The higher wage earner who paid more into CPP during the years the couple was together will see his or her CPP pension reduced. The other, who had lower wages, will benefit from an increase in the amount of pension. Someone who never contributed to CPP can acquire a CPP pension in this way.

40: Are there any tax reduction strategies to use with CPP?

The CPP can be split between spouses; this is called assignment. The CPP of each spouse is added together and apportioned equally between both. Therefore, the CPP of one spouse will be reduced while the CPP of the other is increased.

Splitting the pension only makes sense if there is a discrepancy between the tax rates of each of the two spouses. Both spouses must agree to splitting.

Money received from the Post-Retirement Benefit Plan is not eligible for splitting.

41: If I continue to work after 60, even though I receive the CPP, do I still make CPP contributions?

Both you and your employer will contribute to the Post-Retirement Benefit at the same rate of contribution you made to the CPP. Contributions to age 65 are mandatory, between 65 and 70 they are optional.

If you don't begin a CPP pension and continue to work, you will continue to make contributions as you have done as long as you worked.

42: What are the factors that will contribute to how much I will get in CPP?

There are many factors taken into consideration when determining how much you are going to receive as a benefit.

They include:

- how much you contributed to CPP;

- how long you contributed;

- your age when you begin taking CPP.

43: **I stayed at home to raise my children. Will that affect my CPP?**

Throughout the years you contributed to CPP, up to 7 years of your lowest earnings were automatically dropped from the calculation in order to bring up your average earnings and give you the best possible pension. Starting in 2012, the number of years of lowest earnings was increased to 7.5 and in 2014 the number of years will increase to 8. The result of these increases is a likely small increase to your benefit if you were eligible for CPP in 2012 or later.

44: **What is OAS?**

OAS is the federal pension available to every Canadian who meets requirements as a resident and is not incarcerated in a jail or prison with a sentence longer than two years. It is paid as a full pension or partial pension.

45: **Who gets a full OAS pension?**

You will get a full pension if you lived in Canada for 40 years after turning 18, or you meet the requirements specified for living in Canada.

46: **Who gets a partial OAS pension?**

If you lived in Canada for at least 10 years after age 18 and are living in Canada when you receive your pension, you may qualify for a partial pension. It is paid as 1/40th of the full pension for each year of residence after age 18.

47: When should I start OAS?

Prior to July 2013, the OAS started at age 65 if you applied. On that date, voluntary deferral of the pension to a later date became possible. However, you cannot begin OAS before 65.

The benefit of voluntary deferral is, like the CPP, the OAS pension increases in value every month you don't take it after age 65. The increases continue up to age 70 when the "deferral bonus" stops. The longer you wait, the more you receive on a monthly basis for the rest of your life.

If you do not need the income from the OAS at age 65, defer beginning the pension in order to receive the enhanced benefit.

48: When will I receive OAS and how do I get it?

You will receive the pension:

- the month after you meet the requirements for residence and legal status;

- the month after you turn 65; or

- the month you ask to have the payments start.

In 2023, the pension will no longer be available at age 65. The pension age begins to increase and by 2029 the OAS will not be paid until age 67.

You receive your pension within the last three banking days of every month by cheque or direct deposit. You receive the pension for life unless your taxable income exceeds the limit set by the government.

As an OAS recipient you will receive 100% of the OAS pension providing your net income is less than about $71,000 (in 2013). If your net income puts you in the second bracket of earnings, between $71,000 and about $115,000 (for 2013), part of the OAS pension will have to be repaid to the government. These repayments are usually deducted from your pension before it is issued. When your net income reaches the third bracket, about $115,000, the full OAS is eliminated.

A pension that is reduced or eliminated can be reinstated if income levels drop.

The dollar amounts for the three OAS brackets increase every year.

49: How much more will I get in my OAS by waiting after I'm 65 to start?

After July 2013, you will receive 0.6% per month or 7.2% per year more by waiting, up to age 70. There aren't any more increases after you turn 70.

50: Will I receive the OAS if I continue to work after age 65?

You are entitled to receive the OAS (providing you meet its requirements) regardless of whether you work or not. However, you may find that your net income from working puts you in a position that you lose some or the entire pension because you make "too much".

For most, employment income will far exceed their OAS pension so they are better to work and earn rather than retire in order to receive OAS.

51: How do I declare OAS pension income on my tax return?

Each January you will receive a T4-OAS tax information slip, or an NR4-OAS tax information slip if you are a non-resident of Canada. This shows your pension and tax paid. The slip should be attached to your income tax return.

52: What is the clawback?

The clawback refers to reducing OAS pension due to income being received. This starts to happen when the net income that is being received from all sources reaches $71,000 (in 2013) at which point the OAS is partly repaid. When net income reaches $115,000 (in 2013) the OAS is entirely forfeited. The official name for the clawback is the "Recovery Tax." As noted previously, if income falls, the pension will be reinstated.

53: Will OAS still be paid if I leave Canada?

Your pension will be paid indefinitely while you are outside Canada if you lived in Canada for at least 20 years after turning 18 or you lived or worked in a country that has a social security agreement with Canada and you meet the 20-year residency requirement under the provisions of that agreement and your application is approved.

Otherwise, the pension will be paid for the month you leave and six more months.

54: Does OAS provide a death benefit?

No.

55:   Is my OAS pension taxed?

Yes. The amount you receive from OAS becomes part of your taxable income together with your employment income, and other income you might receive, for instance from a business, or by renting out property.

The OAS recipient receives 100% of the OAS pension providing his or her net income is less than about $71,000 (in 2013). If net income is between $71,000 and about $115,000 (for 2013), part of the OAS pension will have to be repaid. These repayments are usually deducted from the pension before it is issued. When net income is $115,000, the full OAS is eliminated.

56:   How is the amount of my OAS pension determined?

The amount you will receive as an OAS pension will be the result of the amount set by the government for the year, the length of time you lived in Canada, plus any bonus you will be entitled to by deferring your pension if you choose to begin to receive it later than age 65. Deferring your pension is optional, not a requirement.

57:   Will I receive OAS automatically?

No. You should apply six months before age 65 or, if you will be deferring your benefit, six months before you wish your pension to begin.

58:   Who can receive the GIS?

The Guaranteed Income Supplement is received by those who are receiving OAS and whose income meets specifications. It is intended as an income supplement for low-income earners.

59:   How much is received, and when does it start?

The amount received depends on the marital status of the applicant and other income received. It can begin in the same month that OAS begins.

60:   How do you get it?

You must apply for GIS and also reapply every year.

61:   Is the benefit taxable to those who receive it?

No.

62:   Can GIS be paid to someone outside Canada?

It will be paid for six months after a recipient leaves Canada.

63:   Who can receive the Allowance?

The Allowance can be received by the wife or husband of a person who receives OAS, or a surviving spouse. The applicant must also meet the residency requirement. It calls for residence in Canada for 10 years after the age of 18.

The Allowance is paid to those whose income is lower than the amount specified for either a couple when a spouse is applying, or an individual if a survivor is applying.

64:   How much is received?

The formula to determine the amount of benefit is legislated and fairly incomprehensible. Details can be accessed here:

http://www.servicecanada.gc.ca/eng/isp/oas/pdf/
sv-oas-rates-jan-mar-2013.pdf

65:   Is a pension available for war veterans?

The War Veterans Allowance is a monthly allowance for low-income veterans of the Second World War or Korean War, Allied veterans who meet residency requirements, and some civilians who served during the Second World War. The amount received is based on income, marital status, and dependents.

66:   How do I apply for a veteran's pension?

The pension application is made to Veterans Affairs Canada. You can apply online or print out the form and send it in. It is available here:
http://www.veterans.gc.ca/eng/forms/document/429

67:   I live in Alberta. Are any other income benefit programs available for me?

Income programs for Alberta seniors include:

- the Alberta Seniors Benefit (ASB): provides a monthly cash benefit to low- and moderate-income seniors aged 65 and over.

Other programs include:

- Education Property Tax Assistance for Seniors that rebates a portion of the education expense in property taxes;

- Prescription Drug Coverage and Dental and Optical Assistance for Seniors;

- Housing programs.

68: I live in BC. Are any other income benefit programs available for me?

Income programs for BC seniors include:

- Seniors' Supplement: a monthly payment to seniors receiving OAS, and GIS or the Allowance.

Other programs include:

- Shelter Aid for Elderly Renters: financial assistance for those 60 and older whose rent exceeds a certain percentage of their monthly income;

- Property Tax Deferment: for those 55 and older, or who is a surviving spouse, or a person with disabilities, this loan allows someone to defer some or all of the property tax on their principal residence;

- Pharmacare and Medical Services Plan Premium Assistance;

- Bus Pass: a pass is provided for low-income seniors;

- Housing programs.

69: I live in Manitoba. Are any other income benefit programs available for me?

Income programs for Manitoba seniors include:

- the 55 Plus Program provides benefits to those 55 and over who meet the income requirements.

Other programs include:

- School Tax Assistance provides property tax assistance for renters and homeowners 55 and older;

- RentAid that helps low-income seniors pay their rent;

- Seniors Eyeglass Program to help pay for prescription glasses for those 65 and older;

- Housing programs.

70: I live in Saskatchewan. Are any other income benefit programs available for me?

Income programs for seniors in Saskatchewan include:

- the Seniors Income Plan that provides a monthly benefit to low-income seniors 65 and older whose only source of income is OAS and GIS;

- the Saskatchewan Pension Plan (SPP) is a voluntary plan for those between 18 and 71 to save for retirement.

Other programs include:

- the Seniors' Drug Plan for those 65 and older;

- a housing program.

71: I live in Ontario. Are any other income benefit programs available for me?

Income programs for seniors in Ontario include:

- the Guaranteed Annual Income System for Seniors (known as GAINS). It provides a monthly income supplement for those aged 65 and older who receive OAS and GIS and whose income meets guidelines.

Other programs include:

- the Ontario Energy and Property Tax Credit helps low and moderate-income earners with the sales tax that is charged on energy bills and property taxes;

- the Provincial Land Tax Deferral Program for low-income seniors provides a partial deferral of land tax and education tax;

- the Senior Homeowner's Property Tax Grant is provided every year to help offset property taxes for those with low and moderate incomes who own their own homes;

- the Drug Benefit Program to assist with the cost of prescription drugs;

- housing programs.

72: I live in Quebec. Are any other income benefit programs available for me?

There are no supplemental income programs in Quebec. Quebec offers one program to assist with home renovations for seniors 65 and older.

73: I live in Nova Scotia. Are any other income benefit programs available for me?

There is no supplementary income program for seniors in Nova Scotia.

Other programs include:

- a prescription drug plan for those 65 and older;

- a property tax rebate program for a portion of municipal property tax paid in the preceding year;

- a personal alert assistance program that provides up to $480/year to reimburse approved seniors for the purchase of a personal alert assistance service;

- numerous housing programs.

74: I live in New Brunswick. Are any other income benefit programs available for me?

The income program for seniors in New Brunswick is:

- the low-income seniors benefit for eligible low-income seniors.

Other programs include:

- prescription drug coverage;

- numerous housing programs.

75: I live in Prince Edward Island. Are any other income benefit programs available for me?

There is no supplementary income program for seniors in PEI.

Other programs include:

- Senior Citizen Real Property Tax Deferral Program that defers property taxes indefinitely for eligible low-income seniors;

- Many housing programs.

76: I live in Newfoundland and Labrador. Are any other income benefit programs available for me?

There is no supplementary income program for seniors in Newfoundland and Labrador. However there is a low-income seniors benefit (NSB) that is a refundable tax credit for low-income seniors.

Other programs include:

- a prescription drug program;

- a housing subsidy.

77: I live in the Yukon. Are any other income benefit programs available for me?

The income program for seniors in the Yukon is:

- Yukon Seniors' Income Supplement that provides a monthly payment to low-income seniors who receive OAS or GIS and the Allowance.

Other programs include:

- the Pioneer Utility Grant helps seniors 65 and over to offset the cost of utilities;

- a prescription drug plan;

- extended health care;

- housing.

78: I live in Nunavut. Are any other income benefit programs available for me?

The income program for seniors in Nunavut is:

- the Senior Citizen Supplementary Benefit Program to assist those with low incomes.

Other programs include:

- a fuel subsidy for those 60 and older who own their own homes that contributes towards the cost of household heating;

- extended health benefits that in addition to prescription drugs and vision services pay insurance coverage for medical travel.

79: I live in Northwest Territories. Are any other income benefit programs available for me?

The income programs for seniors in Northwest Territories are:

- the Senior Citizen Supplementary Benefit for low-income seniors who receive OAS and GIS;

- the Personal Allowance for those who live in long-term care.

Other programs include:

- extended health benefits for those 60 and older;

- Senior citizens' Motor Vehicle Service Discount that reduces annual fees for vehicle registrations and driver's licenses by 50%;

- Property tax relief to help seniors pay less or no property tax depending on the property that is owned or occupied;

- Home heating subsidy for those 60 and older with low incomes.

PERSONAL RETIREMENT SAVINGS: RRSPS TO RRIFS

This chapter focusses on RRSPs and the conversion options for RRSPs that must be used no later than the end of the year when the RRSP plan owner turns 71. RRIFs are of primary concern.

Questions on other plans, such as LIRAs and LIFS, are covered in the chapter on employer pensions because these plans are only available to those who contributed to an employer pension.

Annuities are covered in insurance and investments.

QUESTIONS:

80. What is a RRIF?
81. Is an RRSP the same as a RRIF?
82. Do I have to open a RRIF with the money in my RRSP?
83. What is the most popular choice for RRSP maturity?
84. What are the differences between an RRSP and a RRIF?
85. Why do most people choose a RRIF?
86. Why would I want a RRIF?
87. Is a RRIF the same as an RRSP?

88. How is the transfer of investments from the RRSP to the RRIF accomplished?
89. What age should I convert my RRSP to a RRIF?
90. Can I make a withdrawal from an RRSP?
91. What are the basics for RRIF withdrawals?
92. What is the minimum RRIF withdrawal based on?
93. Do I have to make a withdrawal from my RRIF every year?
94. Is there a withholding tax on RRIF withdrawals?
95. Are there any restrictions as to who can have a RRIF?
96. How old do you have to be to open an RRSP?
97. How old do you have to be to open a RRIF?
98. When is a RRIF closed?
99. Can I have an RRSP and a RRIF at the same time?
100. Are there disadvantages to having a RRIF?
101. What is the best RRSP maturity option from a tax perspective?
102. What happens to my RRIF when I die?
103. What happens to my RRSP if I die?
104. What if I convert my RRSP to a RRIF and then I receive a sum
    of money I'd like to deposit?
105. When is the last time I can make a deposit to my RRSP?
106. Should I continue to contribute to an RRSP after I am retired?
107. Who can I set my RRIF up with?
108. Is a RRIF protected from claims made by my creditors?
109. How do I know if a RRIF is the right choice for me when
    my RRSP matures?
110. How is my RRIF withdrawal taxed?
111. What if I don't want to receive my minimum RRIF withdrawal as cash?

112.   If minimum RRIF withdrawals are taken, when will the RRIF be totally depleted?
113.   Can I avoid paying tax on my RRIF when I die?
114.   Do I have any options if I transfer my RRSP to a RRIF and I find RRIF management too much?
115.   What happens to a spousal RRSP when the plan owner turns 71?
116.   What is a locked-in RRSP?
117.   What happens to my RRIF if my marriage ends?
118.   Should I pay down debt or contribute to my RRSP?

CHART: RRIF MINIMUM WITHDRAWALS
(following question 118)

HERE ARE THE ANSWERS...

80:   What is a RRIF?

A RRIF is a Registered Retirement Income Fund. It is a
form of pension savings account that pays an annual
income because a minimum amount must be withdrawn
each year. The account is called "registered" because it is
registered by the institution that holds the account, such
as your bank, with Canada Revenue Agency. Because
it is registered, the account provides tax deferral. This
means the value of the account and investment growth
is not declared as income every year. All withdrawals are
declared as income.

81:   Is an RRSP the same as a RRIF?

No. You make contributions to an RRSP; you cannot
contribute money directly to a RRIF. The RRIF is funded
totally and only by transfer of money from another
pension savings plan, such as an RRSP.

82:   Do I have to open a RRIF with the money in
my RRSP?

No. A RRIF is only one of four options available to you if
you are nearing the age when the RRSP must be converted
to another plan. RRSP maturity happens on the last day of
the year in which you turn 71. The four options available
to you are:

• to transfer the money in the RRSP to a RRIF;

71

- to buy an annuity (could be an annuity that will pay you until you are 90; this is called a term certain to age 90 annuity or a life annuity);

- to take the plan value in cash;

- a combination of these things.

83: What is the most popular choice for RRSP maturity?

Transfer of the RRSP account value to a RRIF.

84: What are the differences between an RRSP and a RRIF?

One primary difference is that you cannot deposit money directly into a RRIF.

Also, when you withdraw money from an RRSP you will pay a withholding tax on the total withdrawal. The withholding tax on the RRSP withdrawal represents a portion of what you could owe in income tax when you include the withdrawal in your income for the year.

There is no withholding tax on the minimum annual RRIF withdrawal. There is withholding tax on amounts greater than the minimum.

85: Why do most people choose a RRIF?

A RRIF provides a great deal of income flexibility. There is a minimum amount that must be withdrawn every year, but there is no maximum.

There is also the benefit of holding your savings in an account in which tax is deferred until you make withdrawals. This allows savings to grow tax-free.

Many people believe they can achieve a better return on their savings by making their own investment decisions. The RRIF allows them to do that. It provides all the same investment choices that are available in an RRSP and it is a simple matter just to transfer all the investments and money from the RRSP to the RRIF.

Alas, many choose a RRIF because it is the easiest thing to do. It becomes like an extension of the RRSP and it does not require additional decision-making. This is not a good reason to pick a RRIF over an annuity.

Buying an annuity requires the investments in an RRSP to be sold to accumulate the necessary sum of capital. If your total capital available to buy the annuity is small, you will see in black-and-white the harsh reality of the income you will receive given your sum invested. In fact, this is the same amount you should be taking from your RRIF, no more or the RRIF will run dry.

So, it is a psychological gamble many are willing to take. You can be part of the crowd that goes to RRIFs and self-confident that you can beat the odds and get a better return than the experts who manage annuities. You can also turn a blind eye to the reality of how much you really have saved: it looks like more as a lump sum in a RRIF account than when a monthly annuity payment is received.

But, you do so at your peril; the likelihood of earning a better net return than the experts is remote. Further, you must see the annuity payment as equivalent to what you would get from your RRIF because you don't want your

RRIF to run out of money. An annuity may be a big step and there may be a bit of a learning curve. However, it has two important benefits: an annuity is guaranteed and since no investment decisions are required after it has been purchased, it provides great peace of mind. It eliminates second-guessing. These factors add value.

86: Why would I want a RRIF?

A RRIF defers tax on the money and investments in the account. This is very beneficial because if you withdrew the total value of the RRIF as cash you would pay income tax on that money in the year that you made the withdrawal.

Tax deferral allows the investments in the RRIF to grow on a compound basis: in other words, you get returns on returns.

Also, a RRIF provides flexibility in that there is no maximum to what you can withdraw. So, if you have an unexpected expense, you can take the money you need from the RRIF. This is a major difference between RRIFs and annuities; annuities do not provide any flexibility for withdrawals.

Even though withdrawals from the RRIF are taxed as income regardless of the investments you have in the plan, the ability to hold a wide range of investments in the RRIF gives you the opportunity to earn better returns by investing, for instance, in stocks or bonds. Those returns compound without paying tax.

87: Is a RRIF the same as an RRSP?

A RRIF is the same as an RRSP in the following ways:

1. Income tax is not paid on the balance of either an RRSP or RRIF account each year. For this reason, they are both called tax deferred because tax does not have to be paid until a withdrawal is made. An amount is withheld for tax when money is withdrawn from an RRSP. A RRIF is different from an RRSP because the minimum withdrawal is not taxed when the withdrawal is made. Withdrawals above the minimum have withholding tax.

2. They both charge administration fees to the account owner.

3. They can both be invested in the same wide range of investment products if they are held as self-directed plans. Managed plans offer less investment options.

4. There is no limit on how much can be withdrawn at any time.

5. Withdrawals from the accounts are taxed as income regardless of how the accounts have been invested. Therefore, if you owned a mutual fund that paid dividends and capital gains in your RRSP or RRIF, when you sell those mutual fund units the money you receive is taxed as if it was income; there are no tax advantages for the withdrawn money.

6. Money that is withdrawn from a RRIF cannot be paid back; it can only be paid back to an RRSP if there is unused contribution room.

88: How is the transfer of investments from the RRSP to the RRIF accomplished?

Investments in your RRSP simply rollover to your RRIF. You do not sell your RRSP holdings but just make a transfer from one account to the other.

Likewise, when you withdraw from the RRIF, you can make the withdrawal "in kind" and simply transfer the investment out to a non-registered account or a Tax-free Savings Account.

89: What age should I convert my RRSP to a RRIF?

It depends on your need for income. If you don't want or need payments from your RRIF, then you can delay conversion of your RRSP until the last moment (December 31 of the year you turn 71). If your RRIF is created that day you must begin taking income before your 72nd birthday.

If you need income sooner, convert your RRSP to a RRIF and begin withdrawals.

The key point is: once the RRIF is established, you must begin minimum withdrawals in the following year.

90: Can I make a withdrawal from an RRSP?

You can withdraw from an RRSP in one of three ways:

1. Withdraw money to use as you please. This money cannot be repaid to the RRSP unless you have unused contribution room and then you put back in what you took out. The amount you specify as a

withdrawal will be reduced by what is called a withholding tax. The amount of withholding tax varies by how much you withdraw, and the province you live in.

2. Withdraw money to use as a down payment for a qualified home through the Home Buyer's Plan. The money withdrawn for this use, no more than $25,000, must be repaid over a period of 15 years or it will become a future income tax obligation.

3. Withdraw money for adult education through the Lifelong Learning Plan. Up to $20,000 in total can be withdrawn. The withdrawal must be repaid in 10 years at a minimum of 10% per year of the amount borrowed or it will be added to income tax owing.

91:   What are the basics for RRIF withdrawals?

Very simply, you have to withdraw a minimum amount each year. There are two schedules for withdrawals: one for RRIFs established before 1992 and one for RRIFs established since 1992. We focus on post-1992 RRIFs exclusively. The RRIF withdrawal chart is provided after question 118.

Withdrawals begin the year after the account is opened. If you waited until December 31 of the year you turned 71 to fund your RRIF, you must take the first withdrawal by your 72nd birthday.

A greater percentage of the value of your RRIF must be withdrawn every year --- for instance, at age 65, the minimum percentage is 4%, at age 80 it is 8.75%.

There is no maximum to the amount you can withdraw. However, the more taken, the less remaining! This could be a concern to you if you need the RRIF to align with your planned lifespan.

If you have multiple RRIF accounts, you must withdraw the annual minimum from each account.

92:   What is the minimum RRIF withdrawal based on?

It is based on:

- the market value of the plan as of December 31st of the preceding year;

- your age;

- the percentage of the plan that you must withdraw according to the minimum withdrawal schedule (provided after question 118).

The minimum withdrawal percentage is multiplied by the market value to determine how much you must take out.

Before age 71, the minimum withdrawal is calculated as $1 \div (90 - \text{your current age})$. For instance if you are 64, your minimum withdrawal will be $1 \div (90 - 64) = 1 \div 26 = .038$. Therefore, if your RRIF account value was $100,000, your minimum withdrawal would be $3,800.

However, if your spouse is younger than you are, you can base your minimum withdrawal on his or her age to reduce the amount you must take out. This permanently bases your withdrawals at a lesser amount than if your age was used. This means, if you are only taking out the minimum, you will not deplete the value of the RRIF as quickly as it would be if you were using your age.

93: Do I have to make a withdrawal from my RRIF every year?

Yes. There is a minimum amount that must be withdrawn every year, no matter how old you are.

When you are less than 71, the formula is: 1 (90 – age).

The withdrawal can be based on the age of your younger spouse. The minimum withdrawal amount will be less and you will have less taxable income as a result. Once this decision is made, it is cannot be reversed.

See the withdrawal schedule following question 118.

94: Is there a withholding tax on RRIF withdrawals?

There is no withholding tax on the minimum RRIF withdrawal like there is with an RRSP withdrawal. In other words, if your annual minimum withdrawal is $1,500 you will receive $1,500.

There is a withholding tax on the amount above the RRIF minimum. If you live outside Quebec, you will pay 10% on a withdrawal up to $5,000, 20% on amounts between $5,000 and $15,000, and 30% on amounts over $15,000. Quebec sees the withholding tax rate at 16%, 18% or 21.39%.

For example, if you live outside Quebec and you are required to take $1,200 per year as your minimum withdrawal ($100/month) but you choose to take an additional $6,000 per year ($500/month), the 20% withholding tax will apply to the $500.

All withdrawals must be declared as taxable income even if you have paid the withholding tax.

95: Are there any restrictions as to who can have a RRIF?

You can't have a RRIF if you do not have a pension savings account to roll over to the RRIF, such as an RRSP. An RRSP becomes a RRIF; therefore, no RRSP, no RRIF.

96: How old do you have to be to open an RRSP?

You can open an RRSP at any age but you must have earned income in the year you want to make a contribution or unused contribution room from previous years. Basically, earned income is money you receive from working. Earned income does not include investment income, pension payments, or RRIF payments.

97: How old do you have to be to open a RRIF?

You can open a RRIF at any age. Minimum withdrawals must then begin in the following year.

98: When is a RRIF closed?

A RRIF is closed by one of two events:

1. death of the account owner.

2. total depletion of the account. If all the money in the account is spent, the RRIF is finished.

99: Can I have an RRSP and a RRIF at the same time?

Yes. It is suggested that people with RRSPs should have more than one RRSP and more than one RRIF. You need to withdraw the minimum from every RRIF account every year. However, each minimum can be withdrawn with no withholding tax. With multiple accounts you could find you receive enough money so that you do not need more than the minimums, and you would not have to take extra and pay the holdback.

100: Are there disadvantages to having a RRIF?

The main disadvantage may be how easy it is to take money out without an eye to future needs. People are living longer and they need, or want, their money to last. Taking withdrawals that are a proportionately large amount of your account in the early phase of retirement means less ability to recoup the value of withdrawals from investment growth, and therefore leaves less for the future. Care must be taken so that the money doesn't run out before you do.

Another disadvantage is that all the money you receive from the RRIF must be declared as if it was earned as interest. If you diligently acquired dividend-paying stocks and growth stocks over the period you held the RRIF thinking how you would benefit from the better tax rates applied to dividends and capital gains when the time came to sell the investments and withdraw their value from the RRIF, you will be sorely disappointed. Interest is taxed at your marginal tax rate, the same as income.

101: What is the best RRSP maturity option from a tax perspective?

There is little difference between a RRIF and an annuity from a tax perspective since both are taxable income; cashing out the RRSP is the worst plan of action.

If you took the total account value out in cash, tax would have to be paid on that amount in the year it was taken. Although you could transfer some of that cash to a Tax-free Savings Account so you wouldn't pay tax twice on future growth of the money, you will be subject to the contribution limits of the TFSA. If you have more than what is allowed to go into the TFSA, the cash from your RRIF would have to go into another savings or investment account and you would be taxed on the returns every year. In effect, you would be taxed twice on that money.

102: What happens to my RRIF when I die?

When you set up the account, you can name a successor annuitant, a "qualified beneficiary" to receive the value of the account, a beneficiary, or the proceeds can be paid to your estate after your death.

Your spouse can be a successor annuitant of the RRIF. If so, he or she simply takes over the RRIF and begins to make withdrawals. There will be no fees and no need to sell investments.

A "qualified beneficiary" includes your spouse who can roll the funds into his or her RRIF or RRSP or transfer the funds to an annuity without paying tax. In this case, the investments in the RRIF will be sold and the resulting money is rolled over. There are disadvantages to this plan of action including the fees that will be incurred in collapsing the RRIF and the fact that the investments may be sold at a time when market values are down.

A financially dependent child or grandchild who is dependent because he or she is physically or mentally impaired can also rollover the funds to an RRSP, RRIF, or annuity tax-free. A child or grandchild who is simply financially dependent on the deceased can roll the funds into a term annuity tax-free or transfer it to their RRSP.

A beneficiary can be named to receive the funds tax-free if the tax owing on the money has been declared by the executor for the deceased on, what is called, the final or terminal tax return.

In that case, the amount of tax owing on the RRIF will be based on the tax rate for your estate. The tax for the RRIF will be based on the fair market value of all property held in the RRIF at the time of death plus any withdrawals made in the year of death.

If you have an infirm child or grandchild who is financially dependent on you, the RRIF can also rollover tax-free to the child's Registered Disability Savings Plan.

103: What happens to my RRSP if I die?

The same options are available to RRSP owners as those with RRIFs. However, unique to RRSPs is the ability of your legal representative to make a contribution to your spouse's RRSP up to 60 days after the end of the year in which you die. This gives your estate the benefit of the tax deduction on your final tax return while increasing the value of the spousal plan.

104: What should I do if I convert my RRSP to a RRIF and then I receive a sum of money I'd like to deposit?

If you are younger than age 71, you can open another RRSP to deposit the money if you have earned income on which you can base the contribution or you have available contribution room.

You could also use the money to make a contribution to a spousal RRSP, or deposit the money into a Tax-Free Savings Account.

Finally, you can buy many forms of investments, including annuities, at any age.

105: When is the last time I can make a deposit to my RRSP?

Your last contribution to your own RRSP can be made no later than December 31 of the year you turn 71.

You can continue to make contributions to a spousal plan in the name of your wife or husband until she or he turns 71.

After you die, your legal representative can make a contribution to your spouse's plan up to 60 days after the end of the year in which you die.

106: Should I continue to contribute to an RRSP after I am retired?

If you have income or unused contribution room that permits you to make RRSP contributions, then by all means continue to contribute. You will receive the benefit of the tax deduction and the tax-deferred growth on your contribution.

Remember, income for RRSP contributions cannot be what you receive as investment income, pension benefits, or payments from a RRIF. You must earn income as salary, or from a business, rental properties, research grants, alimony, or royalties to be able to contribute.

107: Who can I set my RRIF up with?

Financial institutions including banks, credit unions, trust companies, caisses populaires, investment dealers, and mutual fund and insurance companies all provide RRIF accounts.

108: Is a RRIF protected from claims made by my creditors?

If the RRIF is opened within 12 months of declaring bankruptcy it can be seized by your creditors. Otherwise, the RRIF is protected from creditor claims.

109: How do I know if a RRIF is the right choice for me when my RRSP matures?

A RRIF is a good choice for you if you have the self-control needed so that you do not deplete the value of the account prematurely.

It is also a good choice if you wish to be involved in investment decisions. If you are comfortable buying and selling investments, then the RRIF will be very suitable for you. If you'd rather not take on the responsibility for those decisions, then an annuity is your better bet.

Finally, a RRIF is your only choice if you wish to invest in certain options, such as stocks.

110: How is my RRIF withdrawal taxed?

The amount you receive is taxed at your marginal tax rate. You can reduce your tax bill by:

- splitting the amount you receive with your spouse (this is only effective if your spouse is in a lower marginal tax bracket than you are);

- basing your withdrawals on the age of your spouse if he or she is younger than you are. In this case, you will receive less as a minimum withdrawal and will therefore have less taxable income.

111: What if I don't want to receive my minimum RRIF withdrawal as cash?

There is no need to take the minimum withdrawal as cash. You can take the withdrawal "in kind." For instance, if you own units of a mutual fund in your RRIF they can be transferred to another account as is. A TFSA or an investment account could be used for this purpose and you will have satisfied the need for your minimum withdrawal.

The benefit of doing the in kind transfer is that you do not have to sell your investment at a time when its market value may be down or there is still a sales charge that would be applied. Sales charges on mutual funds are often deferred so that if the mutual fund is cashed out within a specified number of years after purchase, there is a charge against the value of your investment.

Also, if you owned stocks, you would not have to pay the commission to sell the stock, and if you wanted to rebuy the same stock outside of the RRIF, another commission on repurchase.

You may wish to retain your investment and transfer it in kind simply because it has great future potential.

112: If minimum RRIF withdrawals are taken, when will the RRIF be totally depleted?

Let's put it this way: the money will last longer than you do!

At age 94 you must start taking 20% per year as your minimum withdrawal. Even at age 125 there will still be money remaining in the account for the minimum 20% withdrawal, though it is a moot point since people don't live that long.

113: Can I avoid paying tax on my RRIF when I die?

You could name a charity as a beneficiary and receive a tax credit for 100% of the contribution. This could offset any tax owing on the RRIF.

114: Do I have any options if I transfer my RRSP to a RRIF and I find RRIF management too much?

Yes, you can transfer some or all of your RRIF to a term-certain-to-age-90 annuity at any time. If you were invested in GICs in the RRIF you might have to wait until they mature to transfer the money or you would be penalized for cashing in your GIC early.

115: What happens to a spousal RRSP when the plan owner turns 71?

It becomes a spousal RRIF with the same minimum withdrawal requirements as a non-spousal plan. Please see the Income Tax chapter for more on this subject.

116: What is a locked-in RRSP?

A locked-in RRSP is actually now called a Locked-in Retirement Account (LIRA). It is an account that must be used by those who have locked-in pension savings; those savings are created by contributions to a pension with an employer. On retirement the locked-in savings must be transferred away from the employer and a LIRA is one of the accounts to which the transfer can be made.

A LIRA can only be funded by a pension transfer and no withdrawals are permitted. When the time comes when the money is needed, or no later than the end of the year in which the plan owner turns 71, the money in a LIRA must be transferred to a Life Income Fund (LIF) or Prescribed Retirement Income Fund (PRIF), depending on which province you live in. See the chapter on company pensions for more details on LIRAs/LIFs/PRIFs.

117: What happens to my RRIF if my marriage ends?

The account value must be split according to the regulations of the province you live in.

118: Should I pay down debt or contribute to my RRSP?

The conventional answer is to pay down your debt, including mortgages, first.

However, another approach is to make your RRSP contribution and then apply the tax refund you receive to your debt and/or mortgage.

The amount you receive from your refund will not be as much as the amount you paid into your RRSP unless you have extra deductions and credits that bump up the refund, but you will be killing two birds with one stone.

RRIF MINIMUM WITHDRAWALS

AGE AT THE BEGINNING OF THE YEAR	MINIMUM WITHDRAWAL FOR RRIFs OPENED AFTER 1992 (percentage of the plan value that must be withdrawn)
Less than 71	1 (90 – age)
65 years	4.00%
66 years	4.17%
67 years	4.35%
68 years	4.55%
69 years	4.76%
70 years	5.00%
71 years	7.38%
72 years	7.48%
73 years	7.59%
74 years	7.71%
75 years	7.85%
76 years	7.99%
77 years	8.15%
78 years	8.33%
79 years	8.53%
80 years	8.75%
81 years	8.99%
82 years	9.27%
83 years	9.58%
84 years	9,93%
85 years	10.33%
86 years	10.79%
87 years	11.33%
88 years	11.96%
89 years	12.71%
90 years	13.62%
91 years	14.73%
92 years	16.12%
93 years	17.92%
94 years +	20.00%

YOUR COMPANY PENSION

This chapter is devoted to explaining employer pensions. This is a very complex subject since there are different rules for different kinds of pensions, provincial vs. federal pensions, and between the provinces themselves.

QUESTIONS:

119. What forms of employer pensions are available?
120. How do I know if I have one of these pensions?
121. Why are these plans called "registered"?
122. What is a defined benefit plan?
123. Are pensions from a defined benefit plan an absolutely sure thing?
124. How is the amount of pension I will receive as a defined benefit plan determined?
125. What is a defined contribution plan?
126. Can I still have an RRSP when I have a pension from my employer?
127. How are employer pensions different from saving for retirement in an RRSP?
128. Should I take the commuted value of my company pension?
129. What options are available for me when the time comes to transfer the value of my pension?
130. What is a LIRA?

131. How old do you have to be to set up a LIRA?
132. When does my LIRA have to be closed?
133. Will my LIRA be subject to provincial rules or rules for federal pensions?
134. Why can't I just withdraw the money from my LIRA when I want?
135. Is there any way to get access to my money that is in a LIRA?
136. What is the unlocking age for a LIRA in BC?
137. What is the unlocking age for a LIRA in Alberta?
138. What is the unlocking age for a LIRA in Saskatchewan?
139. What is the unlocking age for a LIRA in Manitoba?
140. What is the unlocking age for a LIRA in Ontario?
141. What is the unlocking age for a LIRA in Quebec?
142. What is the unlocking age for a LIRA in Nova Scotia?
143. What is the unlocking age for a LIRA in New Brunswick?
144. What is the unlocking age for a LIRA in Newfoundland and Labrador?
145. What is the unlocking age for a LIRA in PEI?
146. What are the conditions for financial hardship?
147. Can my federal pension be unlocked?
148. What is a LIF?
149. When can I open a LIF?
150. What happens to my LIRA or LIF if my marriage ends?
151. How is the maximum LIF withdrawal determined?
152. Is the maximum LIF withdrawal ever waived?
153. What's the LIF alternative for those with a federal pension?
154. What is a PRIF?
155. What would be the benefit of transferring my funds to a life annuity?

156.   What would be the benefit of transferring my
        funds to a LIF or PRIF instead of an annuity?
157.   How can I get out from the rules that apply to
        company pensions?
158.   Is there a simple way to explain company pensions?

HERE ARE THE ANSWERS...

119: What forms of employer pensions are available?

Pensions provided to employees by employers are called registered pension plans. They include defined benefit plans, defined contribution plans, hybrid plans, and if legislation is finalized, the Pooled Registered Pension Plan (PRPP).

Far less common are group RRSPs, deferred profit sharing plans, and individual pension plans.

120: How do I know if I have one of these pensions?

It is important not to confuse an employer pension with the Canada Pension Plan as a surprisingly large number of employees have been known to do.

When you are registered in an employer pension you should receive an annual pension statement from your employer. These statements can be confusing so if you have any doubts about the information, you should review the statement with your pension administrator. This may be someone in your human resources department. Otherwise, go to the person you use for professional financial advice.

121: Why are these plans called "registered"?

Such employer pensions are registered with Canada Revenue Agency (CRA) according to the requirements of the pension benefits act of the province in which the company is based. The purpose of registration is so each person enrolled in the plan enjoys the tax advantages bestowed by CRA for company pensions.

122: What is a defined benefit plan?

A defined benefit plan is the gold standard of retirement pensions. Employers and employees contribute and, at retirement, the employee begins to receive a set amount on a monthly basis. That amount may be indexed to inflation and there is typically a survivor benefit.

The plan provides simplified retirement income: the retiree has no investment decisions to make --- he or she gets a monthly cheque, and that's it.

123. Are pensions from a defined benefit plan an absolutely sure thing?

Yes, providing the plan is properly funded on the employer-contribution side. In 2011, two-thirds of companies surveyed by the debt-rating agency DBRS had a "significant margin" of underfunding in their pension plans. One reason for this situation is today's low interest rates and another is due to how much longer people are living. The responsibility for the gap between the amount in the pension fund and the amount needed to actually pay the pensions to retirees rests with the company.

If a company that provided a pension plan to its employees becomes insolvent and its pension is underfunded, the pensioners who had been enrolled in the pension plan will receive less than what had been promised. In some jurisdictions, the government guarantees a minimum income will be received. For instance, in Ontario the Pension Benefits Guarantee Fund insures pensions up to $1,000/month.

124: How is the amount of pension I will receive as a defined benefit plan determined?

The amount you will receive as a pension is a result of which formula your plan is based on. These formulas apply only if you have a defined benefit plan. They include:

- the career average earnings formula. The pension is a certain percentage (not more than 2%) of average earnings multiplied by years' work.

- The final average earnings formula. The pension is a certain percentage (not more than 2%) of the final average or best average earnings for a stated period before retirement multiplied by years' work.

- The flat benefit formula. The pension is a certain amount of benefit multiplied by years' work.

125: What is a defined contribution plan?

This plan, also known as a DCP or money purchase plan, requires contributions by employer and employee but no promises are made as to how much pension will be received.

97

The amount of pension that will be received is the result of:

- contributions made while employed;

- investment returns on those contributions;

- how the money in the plan is invested on retirement

- how much the pensioner withdraws on an annual basis as pension income.

A major issue associated with the defined contribution pension is that it requires investment decisions while employed, at the time of retirement, and during retirement. Many employees refrain from these decisions during the course of their working lives and their contributions go to a default investment offered by the sponsor of the pension plan. The default investment is one that will provide low rates of return, but at least those returns will be guaranteed. Then, at the time of retirement and during retirement, the retiree must decide how to invest the value of his or her plan; the result of this decision will have a significant bearing on how much he or she receives in the years to come.

126: Can I still have an RRSP when I have a pension from my employer?

Yes. Your RRSP contribution room will be reduced by the amount you contribute to your pension.

127: How are employer pensions different from saving for retirement in an RRSP?

The money deposited to a company pension plan is locked-in. If the pension is a defined benefit plan it will pay a guaranteed amount. An RRSP-based pension cannot provide a guaranteed income unless the RRSP is used to buy an annuity.

If the employer pension is a defined contribution plan, it will become a locked-in account, such as a Life Income Fund, in which withdrawals by the retiree must fall between a minimum and a maximum. A pension funded by an RRSP that is converted to a RRIF specifies an annual minimum withdrawal but no maximum.

Withdrawals are prohibited from locked-in accounts until a specified age, unlike an RRSP from which you can take a withdrawal of any amount at any time. The inability to withdraw pension savings from locked-in plans is a source of frustration for many people. Some provinces have addressed this unhappiness by allowing the unlocking of some money at certain times or certain circumstances.

The reason that people can't get their hands on "their" locked-in pension money to spend as they choose is that these pensions are designed to pay an income for life (according to the terms of the plan). If the money is withdrawn and spent, it won't be available to provide that income.

Finally, in some provinces the locked-in pension must be used to buy an annuity at age 80. There is no similar requirement for RRSPs.

128: Should I take the commuted value of my company pension?

The commuted value of a pension is a lump sum taken by an employee or member of a pension plan. The amount received represents the value of the pension if contributions were to remain in the employer pension plan. It must be transferred to a plan that locks-in the funds, such as a LIRA or LIF. Once that transfer is made, you become your own pension manager.

It may be very tempting to take the commuted value of your pension and have, what may be, hundreds of thousands of dollars put into your hands. However, this is not a good choice if you are not comfortable with, or experienced in, dealing with large sums of money to invest, or do not know investment principles and strategies for such large sums.

Consider too that your spouse would continue to receive a pension from your pension plan if you were to die. If you take over the management of your pension money you would want to ensure that your spouse would be provided for, especially if mismanagement of the funds or poor investment returns left an inadequate sum to live on after your death.

129: What options are available for me when the time comes to transfer the value of my pension?

You can transfer the value of your defined contribution plan to a:

- LIRA (Locked-in Retirement Account), or

- LIF (Life Income Fund) or PRIF (Prescribed Retirement Income Fund) depending on the province you live in, or

- a life annuity.

130: What is a LIRA?

A LIRA (Locked-in Retirement Account) is an account that is funded by a transfer of locked-in pension contributions. Those contributions are a result of what you, and perhaps your employer, contributed to your company pension.

You manage the LIRA account and make investment decisions for the money. No withdrawals are permitted from the LIRA except as noted in the following answers about "unlocking" funds. LIRA account balances must be transferred to a LIF (Life Income Fund) or PRIF (Prescribed Retirement Income Fund), or life annuity no later than the end of the year you turn 71.

Those with a federal pension created by working for an employer that is federally regulated must transfer their LIRA to a RLIF (Restricted Life Income Fund).

131: How old do you have to be to set up a LIRA?

There is no requirement; you can be any age.

132: When does my LIRA have to be closed?

At the end of the year in which you turn 71.

133: Will my LIRA be subject to provincial rules or rules for federal pensions?

Pension plans that are federally regulated include aviation, airlines, atomic energy, banks, broadcasting, flour feed and seed mills, telecommunications, interprovincial transportation, marine navigation, shipping, and railways. If you work for a company in these sectors, your pension will fall under the guidelines for a federal pension.

134: Why can't I just withdraw the money from my LIRA when I want?

A LIRA is a holding account --- the in-between point for your company pension, which has been in your employer's hands, and your ultimate source of retirement income (in the form of a LIF, PRIF or RLIF, or a life annuity).

A LIRA is intended to preserve (and grow) the money you transfer to it so that you will have an income after age 71. Many people become frustrated with their inability to get at the money in their LIRA, however the reason it is locked-up is to prevent the money from being spent before retirement. It will be the source of a pension for life.

When you want income from the LIRA you must either transfer it to the options described above and meet the required age for withdrawals in your province, or satisfy one of the exceptional circumstances for withdrawals described below.

135: Is there any way to get access to my money that is in a LIRA?

LIRA money is unlocked if the account owner is no longer a Canadian resident.

Otherwise, each province sets its own rules. Some provinces allow withdrawals when there is financial hardship; some do not. Some permit a portion or all of the funds in a LIRA to be unlocked if the account balance is below a certain dollar amount or there is a shortened life expectancy but, again, this is not true of all the provinces.

136: What is the unlocking age for a LIRA in BC?

There is no unlocking due to financial hardship or to simply access some of the money. It appears the minimum age at which locked-in funds can be obtained is 55 due to one of the following situations:

A LIRA or LIF with a value of $10,220 (in 2013) or less can be unlocked by a person of any age. However, a larger account cannot be split up to satisfy the small dollar threshold.

If you are 65 or older, you can unlock funds if the value of all your locked-in personal pension savings is worth $20,440 (in 2013). You can also unlock funds if you have a shortened life expectancy.

137: What is the unlocking age for a LIRA in Alberta?

A person must be at least 50 years old and at the point of moving funds to a LIF to unlock funds. At that age and stage, up to half the value of the account can be unlocked.

138: What is the unlocking age for a LIRA in Saskatchewan?

There is no unlocking provision in the LIRA except for small value accounts and shortened life expectancy.

However, when funds are transferred from the LIRA to a PRIF (only available in Saskatchewan and Manitoba) there is no restriction on withdrawals.

139: What is the unlocking age for a LIRA in Manitoba?

You can apply to unlock 50% of locked-in funds once you reach age 55 when the funds have been transferred to a PRIF.

There is also the ability to access small amounts or have a shortened life expectancy.

140: What is the unlocking age for a LIRA in Ontario?

There is unlocking due to financial hardship. Ontario has provisions to unlock small accounts, when there is a shortened life expectancy, and when you transfer money into a LIF. You have 60 days after the date of that transfer to withdraw up to 50% of the amount that was transferred.

141: What is the unlocking age for a LIRA in Quebec?

There is no unlocking due to financial hardship or to simply access some of the money. Quebec makes provision for unlocking if the account value is small and the account owner is 65 or older or there is a reduced life expectancy.

142: What is the unlocking age for a LIRA in Nova Scotia?

There is no unlocking due to financial hardship or to simply access some of the money. Nova Scotia makes provision for unlocking if the account value is small and the account owner is 65 or older or there is a reduced life expectancy.

143: What is the unlocking age for a LIRA in New Brunswick?

New Brunswick does not appear to have unlocking provisions.

144: What is the unlocking age for a LIRA in Newfoundland and Labrador?

There is no unlocking due to financial hardship or to simply access some of the money. Newfoundland and Labrador has provisions to unlock small accounts, and when all accounts are below a set dollar threshold and the plan owner is 55 or older.

145: What is the unlocking age for a LIRA in PEI?

PEI does not have pension legislation and so no age is specified.

146: What are the conditions for financial hardship?

Locked-in funds can be unlocked in some provinces for reasons of financial hardship. Financial hardship generally means:

- your income is less than a certain dollar amount;

- you need the money, whether for mortgage or rent, or risk eviction from your home;

- you need the money to pay a deposit for first and last month's rent;

- the money is needed for medical treatment for you, your spouse, or your dependents;

- you need to make home renovations to accommodate a disability or illness.

Check the pension legislation in your province for their specific interpretation.

147: Can my federal pension be unlocked?

You have a federal pension if you work in one of the industries, such as banking, that is federally regulated.

Unlocking is permitted:

- up to a set dollar amount under conditions of financial hardship;

- for those who are 55 or older with small-dollar amount accounts;

- up to 50% of the plan can be unlocked, once only, for those who are 55 or older once the money is in a RLIF (Restricted Life Income Fund). The withdrawal must be made within 60 days of opening the RLIF and the money must be moved from the RLIF to an RRSP or RRIF.

148: What is a LIF?

A LIF is a Life Income Fund. The LIF is created by transferring funds from a LIRA or from a pension plan. It is an account like an RRIF in which tax is deferred until withdrawals are made. LIFs are no longer available in Saskatchewan and Manitoba.

LIFs are not available to those with a federal pension.

There are many similarities between a Registered Retirement Income Fund (RRIF) and a LIF. Both plans have:

- a minimum annual withdrawal requirement;

- the same options available upon death of the plan owner, such as a tax-free roll-over to a spouse;

- a withholding tax applied on withdrawals above the minimum;

- a choice of investment options.

There is a maximum to how much can be withdrawn from a LIF each year. LIFs require the spouse of a plan owner to waive their rights to a joint and last survivor annuity.

You must convert the LIF to a life annuity before the end of the year you turn 80 if you live in Saskatchewan or Newfoundland and Labrador.

149: When can I open a LIF?

A LIF can be opened at any age in Quebec, New Brunswick, and Manitoba. In other provinces, it cannot be opened before the age that the account owner would receive normal pension benefits. This can be as young as 50 in Alberta, or 55 in other provinces.

150: What happens to my LIRA or LIF if my marriage ends?

The account value must be split according to the regulations of the province you live in.

151: How is the maximum LIF withdrawal determined?

The maximum is based on a formula for the provincial pension that governs the pension plan.

Get advice from your pension administrator on the maximum that will apply to you.

152: Is the maximum LIF withdrawal ever waived?

The total balance of the LIF can be withdrawn:

- in Alberta at age 85;

- in Ontario and New Brunswick at age 90;

- for federal pensions at age 90.

153: What's the LIF alternative for those with a federal pension?

A pension that is federally regulated must be transferred to a RLIF (Restricted Life Income Fund). It is similar to a

LIF but allows a one-time transfer of 50% of the value of the plan to an RRSP or RRIF within 60 days of opening the RLIF.

154: What is a PRIF?

A Prescribed Retirement Income Fund (PRIF) is available only to registered pension plan members whose plans are subject to the Pension Benefits Act in Saskatchewan and Manitoba.

A PRIF is one of the options available to those who:

- have a defined contribution plan that must be transferred from the employer at retirement, or

- have a Locked-in Retirement Account (LIRA) or Locked-in Retirement Savings Plan (Locked-in RRSP), and who need to close down their locked-in plans at age 71.

A minimum amount must be withdrawn annually from the PRIF, but there is no maximum. There is no requirement to ever transfer funds from the PRIF to a life annuity.

155: What would be the benefit of transferring my funds to a life annuity?

You will know how much income you will receive every year until you die. You are also released from making investment decisions, which can bring great peace of mind.

156: What would be the benefit of transferring my funds to a LIF or PRIF instead of an annuity?

You can control how the money is invested and take advantage of investment opportunities as they arise. You can also control the amount of your withdrawals providing you meet the minimum requirement and do not exceed the maximum.

157: How can I get out from the rules that apply to company pensions?

You can emigrate from Canada.

Some provinces will allow depletion of the funds if you are experiencing financial hardship or the account value falls below the threshold amount.

158: Is there a simple way to explain company pensions?

Yes, but be aware that accuracy is in the details. The following overview has many exceptions but it's a handy rundown of the plans:

A Defined Benefit Plan = a life annuity.

A Defined Contribution Plan (DCP) = an RRSP;
An RRSP becomes a RRIF which pays retirement income. Whereas a DCP becomes a LIRA, LIF, PRIF, or annuity, and then retirement income is received from the LIF, PRIF or annuity.

HOME SWEET HOME

This chapter provides the questions and answers that revolve around owning real estate and how you can access and use the equity in that real estate to create retirement income.

QUESTIONS

159. Is it better to own your home or rent when you are retired?
160. I always thought I was saving for retirement by paying off my mortgage. How can I invest my home equity to create retirement income?
161. What are the benefits of owning a condo when you're retired?
162. Are there any disadvantages to owning a condo?
163. Can I leave my house unattended when I go away?
164. How can I produce income from my real estate during retirement?
165. What is a reverse mortgage?
166. What is the cost of a reverse mortgage?
167. Will I pay tax on my home when I sell it?
168. Will I pay tax on my cottage when I sell it?
169. What is the advantage of a reverse mortgage over a home equity line of credit?

170. What is the advantage of a home equity line of credit over a reverse mortgage?

171. How much of the value of my home could I access as a home equity line of credit?

172. Are there tax consequences for a reverse mortgage or a home equity line of credit?

173. Are there tax consequences to renting out my property in Canada?

174. Do I have to declare money I made from renting out my house in the US on my income tax?

175. Is there a way to avoid paying capital gains tax on the sale of my cottage?

176. Can I use the value in my cottage for a home equity line of credit?

177. If I sell some property what should I do with the money?

178. Will I pay capital gains tax when I sell my property in the US?

179. What happens to my real estate when I die?

180. What kind of life insurance should I have if I am going to use it to pay capital gains tax on property?

181: How much life insurance will I need to pay the capital gains on the cottage?

182. Can I donate land I own to charity and receive tax benefits?

HERE ARE THE ANSWERS...

159: Is it better to own your home or rent when you are retired?

The answer to this depends on your need for the equity you have built up in your home. If your sources of retirement income can pay all your bills and provide the lifestyle you want, then there is no overriding reason to sell until you get to the point that the property is too much physical or financial upkeep or you simply want to live elsewhere.

Property ownership entails many hidden costs beyond the mortgage, utility costs, and property taxes. It is estimated that maintenance costs on a newer home should be budgeted at 3.6% of market value per year; those for an older home at 4.5%. These costs may be the ones that make renting or condo ownership appear very attractive.

160: I always thought I was saving for retirement by paying off my mortgage. How can I invest my home equity to create retirement income?

You aren't alone if you are of the view that the equity in your home is your retirement nest egg. An important consideration of this approach is: if you sell your home, where will you live? You can move to a smaller home (and have a correspondingly smaller equity nest-egg remaining because you have had to use some money to buy the smaller home), you can move to a community with lower home prices and property costs, such as taxes (still using some of the equity from the sale), or you can rent.

113

Whatever remains as the lump sum received from the sale of your home after you are re-established in other living quarters must be invested in a way that you can receive money on a regular and sustainable basis --- that is the income stream formed from the home equity.

Some of your best bets to create and sustain that income stream will be an annuity, a laddered portfolio of investments that mature at different times, controlling the rate at which you use the money, or by investing in rental real estate.

- The home equity can become the principal used to buy an annuity. The annuity pays out a combination of that capital plus interest to create a regular income; the interest part of the annuity payment will be taxable. An annuity can be paid out over a period of time, over the life of one person, or for the lifetime of a couple (called a joint and last survivor annuity).

- Laddering is a technique in which investments, such as GICs, mature at different dates so that if interest rates fall, for instance, the investments do not all have to be reinvested at the same low rate. Also, laddering splits up the total amount of home equity being invested so that investment maturity dates align with income needs.

- Controlling the rate at which you use the lump sum from the sale of your property will be essential to create the income stream and ensure it lasts. You have to analyze your expenses to understand how you spend money so that if you have to start reducing costs, you will know what can be cut with the least amount of pain.

The objective is to ensure you can live comfortably using a "safe withdrawal rate" on this principal combined with your other sources of income. The safe withdrawal rate is the amount you can "safely" withdraw each year and maintain an income for life. It is deemed to be no more than 4% of your principal invested.

- Rental real estate could be an option if the home equity was sufficiently large to buy an income property outright. Rent received by you forms your income stream (to be declared as income for tax purposes) and meanwhile the equity in the rental property will be available to you when the property is sold. That sum will be a capital gain.

161: What are the benefits of owning a condo when you're retired?

A condo provides the same ability for increase in value as owning a house. If the condo is your principal residence that increase in market value will be received by you tax-free when you sell. You also have the ability to lock the door and leave for absences without the worry of having someone to check the home regularly. You will also have fewer worries about home break-ins, vandalism, and property upkeep.

Many also look to condos as investments: an owner receives monthly rental income that can pay the mortgage and condo fees, and the equity that builds up is returned to the owner when the condo is sold in addition to any increase in the market value of the unit. Both the rental income and increase in value when selling will have tax consequences. It is best to review condo investing with a tax specialist before buying.

162: Are there any disadvantages to owning a condo?

Monthly condo fees cover the utility costs of your unit and the maintenance fees for the building. A portion of those fees is set aside as a contingency fee to cover exceptional costs, such as a new roof. If repairs need to be done to the building that cannot be covered by the amount retained in the contingency fund, then you can receive a special assessment. This will be a one-time charge for the single repair. However, you can receive more than one special assessment if, for instance, the building is older and needs major ongoing repairs. Even one special assessment can run into many of thousands of dollars. Insurance is available to cover special assessments.

163: Can I leave my house unattended when I go away?

For property insurance purposes, a house cannot be left entirely unattended unless you are prepared that a claim you submit due to the property being empty will not be paid. In other words, if your pipes break because the house was unoccupied and not being checked, your claim may be denied.

If you will be away for less than 30 days, you do not need to tell your insurance company. However, you need to have a competent person check inside every day or two, especially during heating season to ensure the furnace is working properly.

If you are away for longer than 30 days, you must inform your insurance company. They will tell you if you need a special permit to leave the home empty. You will still need to arrange for checking every two days or so, and it may be a good idea to drain water pipes and install a security system.

116

164: How can I produce income from my real estate during retirement?

Here are your options:

1. sell your property and use the proceeds to live on;

2. mortgage the property;

3. rent or lease out the property;

4. get a home equity line of credit;

5. acquire a reverse mortgage.

Selling, mortgaging, and earning rental income, such as you'd get by renting out your property, are things you can do at any age. So is taking out a home equity line of credit, also called a HELOC. A reverse mortgage however is only available to those who are 55 or older.

165: What is a reverse mortgage?

A reverse mortgage returns up to 40% of a home's market value to its owner(s) in regular monthly payments or as a lump sum. It is only available to those who are 55 or older.

It is the opposite of a traditional mortgage: instead of paying for a traditional mortgage, you receive the money every month, or once in a large lump sum.

The amount paid to the homeowner is deducted when the property is sold.

166: What is the cost of a reverse mortgage?

The amount received by the homeowner is treated as a loan and interest is charged on that loan. The interest rate is higher than either a traditional mortgage or a line of credit. The interest costs compound as long as they remain unpaid and can add up significantly.

Reverse mortgages also require the payment of a home appraisal fee, a lawyer, and closing costs of approximately $1,500. There can be stiff penalties for early loan repayment, much as with a traditional mortgage.

167: Will I pay tax on my home when I sell it?

No – your principal residence can be sold tax-free using the "Principal Residence Exemption" providing it does not appear that you are "flipping" properties to make money on their sale.

168: Will I pay tax on my cottage when I sell it?

The proceeds of selling a property that is not your principal residence will be taxed as a capital gain. The amount owing will also depend on when the property was purchased. Since 1982 it is no longer possible for two spouses to claim separate ownership of joint properties; each property owned by one of them is treated as shared marital property and capital gains must be paid on the sale of the property that is not the principal residence. The amount of capital gains tax for a property bought since 1982 will be determined as:

(Market price minus adjusted cost base of property) x 50% x your marginal tax rate.

For instance, if you bought a cottage in 1995 for $100,000 and sold it in 2012 for $250,000, your tax situation would roughly be:

($250,000 - $100,000) x 50% x your marginal tax rate = tax owing

169: What is the advantage of a reverse mortgage over a home equity line of credit?

Reverse mortgage payments can be received monthly so if you feel you might mismanage a large sum of money, such as you would have access to with a home equity line of credit, then the reverse mortgage could be useful. However, that advantage would be lost if you took the reverse mortgage as a lump sum.

A home equity line of credit also requires regular payments to keep the lending institution happy. A reverse mortgage only sees money coming in; it doesn't need repayment until the property is sold.

170: What is the advantage of a home equity line of credit over a reverse mortgage?

Interest charges are far lower with a home equity line of credit than a reverse mortgage.

171: How much of the value of my home could I access as a home equity line of credit?

The maximum amount of loan available, as of 2013, is 65% of a property's value when the loan is taken through a financial institution that is federally regulated, such as the big banks. Financial institutions that do not fall under federal regulations, such as credit unions, can offer a HELOC up to 80% of the value of the home.

172: Are there tax consequences for a reverse mortgage or a home equity line of credit?

No.

173: Are there tax consequences to renting out my property in Canada?

Yes. You must declare the income on your Canadian tax return.

174: Do I have to declare money I made from renting out my house in the US on my income tax?

Yes; you must declare worldwide income on your Canadian tax return. A foreign tax credit may be claimed that is equal to the lesser of the U.S. tax paid and the Canadian tax on that income.

The US tax is 30% of the amount you receive as rent. If you pay this directly to the Internal Revenue Service you do not need to file a US tax return. Alternatively, you can choose to file a US return for the rental income you earn.

175: Is there a way to avoid paying capital gains tax on the sale of my cottage?

One way of getting around capital gains tax on the cottage, or any second property, is to designate it as the principal residence. This is feasible if you sell your home and move into rental accommodation or move to a home that would carry a lower tax liability if it was deemed the second residence.

176: Can I use the value in my cottage for a home equity line of credit?

Yes. The second property can be used for its market value via a home equity line of credit; all requirements must be satisfied to show that the minimum payment on the loan can be made. The amount borrowed on the line of credit must be repaid if the property is sold or the title is transferred.

177: If I sell some property what should I do with the money?

You should use proceeds first to pay off any debts you have: credit cards, loans, and/or any other mortgage. The balance can be invested to either:

- create income.

- create an estate, or make your estate larger.

You could also use the funds to make a gift during your lifetime to children, or grandchildren by funding a Registered Education Savings Plan.

178: Will I pay capital gains tax when I sell my property in the US?

There is a non-resident withholding tax of 10% of the gross sales price of US real estate. Canadians must also file a US tax return in the year the property is sold. You may request to have the withholding tax applied to the net capital gain instead of the gross sales price by filing form 8288-B with the I.R.S. and obtaining a withholding certificate.

If you are selling in order to buy another property in the US, you must still declare and pay US capital gains tax. The capital gain on the property must also be declared on your Canadian tax return though it may be offset via the foreign tax credit by the amount of the capital gain tax paid to the U.S.

If the value of your worldwide estate when you die is less than $3.5 million, including your principal residence, then you will not have to pay US estate or capital gains tax.

Seek tax advice from someone knowledgeable about both the US and Canadian tax regimes if you are the owner of property in the US.

179: What happens to my real estate when I die?

If you have a spouse, your principal residence rolls over to your spouse without tax consequences. A second property, such as a vacation home, will also rollover without probate or capital gains tax if it is held as joint tenancy with right of survivorship (JTWROS).

If you are the second-to-die, your principal residence can be sold or the title transferred tax-free. If a mortgage or reverse mortgage was in place, or there was a line of credit using the home as collateral, such debt would have to be repaid before the property could be transferred.

The title on other properties, such as a cottage, can also be transferred to another person once the legal representative of your estate has paid capital gains tax owing on the property. This is an instance in which life insurance can be vitally important to keep a cottage in the family since the proceeds of the policy can be used to pay the capital gains tax.

180: What kind of life insurance should I have if I am going to use it to pay capital gains tax on property?

You must have life insurance that is guaranteed to be in force at the time of your death. Since no one knows when they are going to die, term life insurance is usually not appropriate since term life policies become very expensive with age. After a certain age (depending on the life insurance company) term life insurance will not be available. If a term policy has lapsed at the time of your death, nothing will be paid to the beneficiary of the policy.

Therefore, you need a type of permanent life insurance policy since permanent life insurance is in force until you die, at whatever age that may be. One type of permanent life insurance called term-to-100 has the lowest premium cost relative to the death benefit. It is a good choice for this use.

181: How much life insurance will I need to pay the capital gains on the cottage?

The formula for the capital gains tax for a property acquired since 1982 will be: fair market value of the property minus its adjusted cost base (basically, what you paid to buy the cottage) equals the capital gain; divide this sum in half and multiply the balance by the marginal tax rate you anticipate on your final tax return (completed after your death). The final sum will be the capital gains tax. This would be the minimum amount you would want as life insurance for this purpose. You would also want to keep an eye on the market value of the property. If you anticipate it will increase, you would want to ensure your life insurance death benefit kept pace since as the market value grows so, too, will the capital gain tax.

Life insurance can be acquired to pay the capital gains tax as we have described. However, to equalize an inheritance between children you would want a higher death benefit than what would be required to pay the capital gains tax alone. For instance, if your son got the cottage and you wanted your daughter to receive an equivalent amount of money after your death, you would have life insurance naming your son as beneficiary in an amount equal to the capital gains tax and an amount naming your daughter as beneficiary equal to the fair market value of the cottage plus the capital gains tax.

182: Can I donate land I own to charity and receive tax benefits?

The Ecological Gifts Program of Environment Canada provides a way for Canadians who own ecologically sensitive land to protect natural areas and leave a legacy for future generations.

The Program created special tax relief for donations of such land, in addition to easements, covenants and servitudes on ecologically sensitive land.

The ecological gift is made by the donor to environmental charities approved by Environment Canada, as well as to any level of government in Canada.

Those who receive the gift are called the recipients. Of course, Environment Canada –in addition to being the administrator of the program—is itself a qualified recipient.

When the donor has identified land that he or she would want preserved, Environment Canada certifies the land is ecologically sensitive, approves the recipient, and certifies the fair market value of the gift. In addition to the charitable donations tax credit (for individuals) and the charitable donations deduction (for corporations), donations certified under the Ecological Gifts Program will no longer be subject to tax on any capital gains accruing in respect of the property.

See **www.ec.gc.ca/pde-egp for more information.**

LIFE INSURANCE

These questions about life insurance cover some issues of enormous importance to Canadians, such as how to extract policy cash values during life, the need for health insurance when travelling to the US (how to make sure your claim won't be denied!), and the need for long-term care insurance.

QUESTIONS

183. What relevance does life insurance have to retirement income?
184. Should I have life insurance when I am retired?
185. How can I use my life insurance policy for income?
186. Can I withdraw money from my life insurance policy?
187. What is a policy loan?
188. What is the cash surrender value of a policy?
189. What is annuitization?
190. Is there any way to receive income from my policy and still leave a legacy?
191. Could I use my life policy as collateral for a loan?
192. Can I convert my term life insurance policy to permanent life insurance?
193. Does term insurance have use for income?
194. When is term insurance no longer available?

215.   What is an annuity rate?
216.   How does an annuity work?
217.   How much does it cost to buy an annuity?
218.   Are there any disadvantages to annuities?
219.   Where can I buy an annuity?
220.   Are annuities still relevant with today's low
       interest rates?

██

HERE ARE THE ANSWERS...

183: What relevance does life insurance have to retirement income?

Life insurance can provide retirement income and can protect assets. Life insurance policies with cash values, such as whole life insurance or universal life insurance, can be used for policy loans. Universal life insurance is unique in that a withdrawal can be made from the policy without terminating the policy. Both types of policy can also be surrendered for their cash value.

One of the traditional and still entirely valid uses for life insurance is to pay last expenses: funeral and other costs incurred on death. This is an important use for life insurance and can save the estate many thousands of dollars so that the estate or a survivor is saved these expenses.

If one or both spouses continue to work past the age at which they might have retired, the income of one or both may be important to "pay the bills." If one of those spouses should die, that source of income will be lost. Life insurance proceeds can replace that lost income.

Life insurance is also available as accident and sickness insurance, called A&S insurance. Two types of A&S are very important for retirees: travel insurance and long-term care insurance (LTCI).

- Travel insurance in the form of health insurance is vital when travelling outside Canada and no one ---

of any age--- should consider even setting foot over the US border without it.

- Long-term care insurance provides money to pay for care when a person is no longer completely able to physically look after himself or herself, or has cognitive impairment, such as Alzheimer's Disease. This product is particularly important for women because they live longer than men and may need care to be provided once they are widowed.

Finally, life insurance companies are a provider of annuities: an investment designed to make payments that can replace or supplement income. An annuity requires a contribution of capital and then pays back that capital plus interest to the person named as annuitant in the contract.

184: Should I have life insurance when I am retired?

The question is not really "should I?" but more like "how much?" This is because most people will find they need insurance and the real issue is to determine how much is needed for what purpose.

If you are using it just to pay final expenses such as your funeral or cremation and burial costs, you may not need more than $20,000. If your estate can handle the expense, you might not need insurance for this purpose.

If debt payment would be required because you have a mortgage or credit card balances, that amount should be added to final expenses. You will also want to add your final income tax bill to the amount estimated for final expenses.

If you return to the workforce after retirement or as long as you continue to work, you would probably want life insurance to replace the value of your income for your surviving spouse if you died. For this, you will need an estimate of the value of your income that would be lost. A life insurance agent can help with this and you will also find calculators online to determine the appropriate sum.

Finally, if you are using life insurance for estate planning purposes, such as paying capital gains tax on property or providing bequests to heirs, you and a tax expert will need to estimate your tax liability at death so that heirs receive their bequests free and clear.

185: How can I use my life insurance policy for income?

You can:

- take the cash surrender value of the policy and invest it in such a way that the lump sum is converted into an income stream;

- take a policy loan from the policy and use that money to fund ongoing expenses;

- make a withdrawal from a universal life insurance policy and use the withdrawal as if it was being received as income;

- receive dividends in cash if you have a participating whole life insurance policy;

- create an insured annuity from a combination of a life annuity with a life insurance policy;

- use it for a leveraged deferred compensation plan if it is a universal life policy.

186: Can I withdraw money from my life insurance policy?

If you have a universal life insurance policy, you can make a withdrawal without canceling or forfeiting the policy. This is the only type of life insurance policy that permits a withdrawal but still continues to provide coverage.

The withdrawal does not need to be repaid and if it is not repaid the amount will be deducted from the death benefit.

The withdrawal, or part of the withdrawal, may be taxable income in the year it is received. This will depend on the adjusted cost basis (ACB) of the policy; the insurance agent or company that issued the policy can best advise you on this issue.

187: What is a policy loan?

When premiums are paid to a whole life insurance policy or a universal life insurance policy a portion of the premiums forms what is called the cash reserve. A policy loan draws upon that cash reserve in order to make a loan from the insurance company to the policy owner.

The maximum amount that can be borrowed is 90% of the cash reserve. The loan does not have to be repaid but if it is not it will be deducted from the death benefit, plus interest.

There may be an income tax cost of the loan; that will be determined by the amount paid in premiums and the amount of the loan. A life insurance agent or tax specialist can best advise on this issue.

188: What is the cash surrender value of a policy?

A cash surrender value is the amount of money a policy owner can receive from the life insurance company if he or she no longer wants his or her policy and exchanges insurance coverage for a lump sum of cash.

The amount to be received by the policy owner will be specified by the life insurance company that issued the policy. It is non-negotiable.

The cash surrender value may be taxed depending on the adjusted cost basis of the policy. The adjusted cost basis is basically what you have paid in premiums.

189: What is annuitization?

Annuitization is when the cash surrender value of a life insurance policy is converted to an annuity. In this way, an income is created from a lump sum amount of money.

Tax will have to be paid as if the policy was surrendered unless the policy owner is totally and permanently disabled.

190: Is there any way to receive income from my policy and still leave a legacy?

Yes, by creating what is called an insured annuity.
An insured annuity is a combination of a life insurance policy with an annuity. Its purpose is to provide you with an income while it simultaneously protects the value of your estate against the steady erosion that would occur if the value of the estate was being used to pay the bills.

How it works:

- You apply for a permanent life insurance policy in the amount you wish as to leave as an estate. A term-to-100 insurance policy is a good choice. It is essential to apply for the insurance before you buy the annuity.

- Then, once approved for the life insurance, you buy a life annuity. The capital you sink into the annuity must be large enough so that the amount you receive as the annuity payment will pay the life insurance premium (at a minimum).

Here's an example:

- Joe wants to leave a $500,000 inheritance to his son.

- He acquires a term-to-100 life insurance policy with a death benefit of $500,000 and names his son as the beneficiary of the policy.

- Once he has the life insurance in place (it is very important to get the life insurance policy first), Joe then proceeds to buy a life annuity that will pay $30,000 a year. He pays the premium for his life insurance policy from the sum he receives from the annuity.

- During his lifetime, Joe can count on the $30,000/ year in income and when he dies, his son will receive $500,000 tax-free. In this way, Joe enjoys the value of his estate during his lifetime and still leaves the desired amount of inheritance for his son.

191: Could I use my life policy as collateral for a loan?

This strategy is called a leveraged deferred compensation plan. A leveraged deferred compensation plan is also known as an insured retirement plan. It is based on using up to 95% of the account value of a universal life insurance policy as collateral with a lending institution. The lender provides a loan, which is tax-free, based on the collateral that exists in the value of the policy. When the policy owner dies, the death benefit of the policy is used to pay off the principal and interest on the loan.

This strategy avoids the tax that would be due if a withdrawal was made from the account value of the policy.

192: Can I convert my term life insurance policy to permanent life insurance?

You can convert your term policy to permanent life insurance if you have a convertible term policy. There will be no need for a medical exam. The amount of insurance can be the same as or less than the original term policy. Premiums will cost more because you will be older than when you first took out the term policy.

If you are unsure whether your term policy is convertible, simply ask your agent or the company that issued your policy.

If you don't have a convertible term policy, you will need to acquire a new permanent life insurance policy and then cancel your term policy or replace the term policy with a permanent policy. There are very specific rules that apply to policy replacement so be aware that your agent will ask you many questions before proceeding.

193: Does term insurance have use for income?

No.

194: When is term insurance no longer available?

Term insurance is life insurance that is designed to protect against premature death; it is not intended to provide protection against death from old age. Therefore, term insurance becomes scarce and expensive as one becomes older.

The age at which term insurance is no longer available depends on the insurance company: it could be age 70, 75, or even 80. Health conditions could preclude a policy from being issued even before age 70.

Premiums become extremely expensive with age because of the greater likelihood that the insurer will have to pay the death benefit.

195: How can I replace my term life insurance with a permanent life insurance policy?

You can do this with a life insurance agent. Make certain that you do not cancel the term life policy until the permanent life policy is in force; if you died when one was cancelled and the other had not been issued, a death benefit would not be paid.

196: I can't afford my premiums any more. Do I have any options other than surrendering my policy?

If you have a term life insurance policy, you can stop paying the premiums while you source out other options. The policy will be cancelled and you will not receive either a refund of what you've paid or any payment if you should die. However, if you die in the period of time between the term policy you cancelled and any new policy being issued, there wouldn't be any death benefit. For this reason, it is wise to find and put in place a new policy before you let the old one go.

Options for term policy owners could include:

- another term life insurance policy with a lower death benefit that would have lower premiums;

- low-cost insurance such as that provided by insurance companies that do not require a medical exam.

If you have whole life insurance, you have several options that will eliminate premiums. They are:

- Using the cash surrender value of the policy to buy extended term insurance. In this case, the whole life policy becomes term insurance that is paid up; that means there are no premiums to pay. The death benefit will be the same as the whole life policy but the term of the policy will be determined by your age at the time the switch is made. For example, if your policy benefit was $250,000 when it was whole life insurance, the new policy will also have a face amount of $250,000. But, the new policy is a term policy and you might find the term is three years. If you died after three years, the face amount wouldn't be paid.

- Using the cash surrender value of the policy to buy a whole life policy that is paid up. In this case, one whole life insurance policy replaces the other. The new one does not require premiums to be paid. The death benefit will be lower than the original policy. For instance, your policy had a face amount of $250,000. You make the switch to a paid-up policy but the face amount will now be $35,000.

197: What are the income-for-life plans I've seen advertised?

These plans are known as Guaranteed Minimum Withdrawal Benefit Plans (GMWBs) or Guaranteed Lifetime Withdrawal Benefit Plans (GLWBs). They are offered by a few life insurance companies to provide a guaranteed income with the potential for capital appreciation.

Such plans require you to deposit money with the insurance company offering the product. Your money is invested in one of the insurer's segregated funds. Withdrawals can begin immediately or deferred to a later date. If they are deferred, you receive a bonus for every year you do not make a withdrawal.

When withdrawals begin, they will be paid over a specified number of years or for life. The amount received as a withdrawal is the higher of either a guaranteed minimum amount or the market value of the segregated fund in which the plan owner has invested. The guaranteed minimum or market value is reset periodically, often every three years. This has the potential to see the withdrawals increase over time.

When you die, your beneficiaries receive the market value of your investment.

These plans are renowned for their complexity and you should make sure you completely understand their details before investing. Read all sales literature very carefully and ask lots of questions so you know what you're buying.

198: Should I buy insurance online or from an insurance company that proclaims "no medical exam is needed" or that "no one is turned down"?

You could, providing that you understand what you are buying. You would also want to ensure that the company is a member of The OmbudServices for Life and Health Insurance [OLHI], a national independent complaint resolution and information service for consumers of Canadian life and health insurance products.

No one is turned down for policies that guarantee acceptance because the death benefit is not paid until after a specified period of time, such as two years. Regular life insurance will pay the death benefit of a policy from day one so long as death is not due to suicide. Suicide is not covered for the first two years of a policy.

Also, the maximum amount that is available as a death benefit is much lower from such companies than traditional insurers. If you need life insurance for estate planning purposes, the sum on offer may simply be insufficient.

Finally, you should always shop around. Get a quote from a company from which insurance is guaranteed, and get at least one quote from an insurance company from which acceptance is not guaranteed (that is, from a traditional life insurance company directly or from a life insurance broker). Also, consider using both sources: the guaranteed-acceptance company to pay final expenses, and the non-guaranteed to pay estate costs. You will only know if this strategy is effective from a cost point-of-view by comparison shopping.

199: What kind of insurance do I need for final expenses?

Final expenses are the expenses that are incurred on death. They include a funeral, burial or cremation, legal and accounting fees, and income tax due for the year of death. Final expenses do not typically include how much you wish to leave as bequests.

Life insurance to pay final expenses must be a form of permanent insurance, not term insurance. This is because you just don't know when you're going to die. You could die at age 70 or age 100. Even though you might have term insurance at age 70, you definitely wouldn't want it at age 100 because (even if you could get it, and you couldn't) the premium cost would be astronomical. So, permanent insurance provides the certainty of being in place no matter what age you die.

Permanent insurance is available as whole life insurance, universal life insurance, and term-to-100 insurance. Term-to-100 has the lowest premium cost relative to coverage.

200: Should I include my life insurance policies in my will?

No. Your will does not need to include mention of your life insurance policy and its beneficiary or beneficiaries.

201: If I want to change my beneficiaries of my life insurance policy, should I do that in my will?

No. You should inform the life insurance company that issued your policy in writing of the change you wish to make. You have no need to tell your beneficiary of the change.

202: How is life insurance used for estate planning?

Life insurance is used in the context of estate planning to pay taxes due on death and to equalize inheritances.

For instance, if a cottage is to be inherited by your child, then a life insurance policy death benefit could be made payable to the child in the amount of capital gains tax that would be due in order to inherit the property tax-free.

If you have two children and the cottage was to be inherited by one of them, then life insurance proceeds could be used to pay the capital gains tax on the cottage. Your child that inherits the property would receive it tax-free. To equalize what that child is receiving, your other child (or children) who doesn't receive the cottage would receive from the life insurance proceeds an amount that is equivalent to the value of the property and the amount that represents the capital gains tax. For instance, Andrea is getting the cottage worth $450,000 and $75,000 from her mother's life insurance policy to pay the capital gains tax on the transfer of the cottage after her mother dies. Andrea's brother, Luke, will get $525,000 from the life insurance policy. Therefore, just to equalize the inheritances, the policy needs to have a death benefit of $600,000.

Life insurance is often used, on the same basis, to equalize inheritances when a business owner leaves a business to one child and an equivalent amount of money (the value of the business) to the other child or children in the family.

203: How can I structure my life insurance policy so that the money will be used to settle expenses after I die?

You name your estate as your beneficiary in the policy. The death benefit of the policy will be paid to the estate and the money will be subject to probate fees according to the probate fee schedule of the province you live in. You also expose the death benefit to creditor claims.

204: Can I access any of the death benefit of my life insurance policy during my lifetime?

Some insurers will advance a small portion of the death benefit of a life insurance policy as a living benefit if there is medical proof that you have a terminal illness and are expected to die within a short period of time. The agent or company that issued the policy can advise on this issue.

The amount received will be deducted from the final death benefit plus interest.

If you live in Saskatchewan, New Brunswick, Nova Scotia, or Quebec you could look for a company that provides viatical settlements.

205: What is a viatical settlement?

A viatical settlement is one of two things.

1. For a person with a life insurance policy, a viatical settlement, also sometimes called a life settlement, is when a person trades in his or her life insurance policy for cash to a company that specializes in these sorts of arrangements. The policy owner receives the money to use as desired. The company that buys the policy continues to pay the policy premiums and then receives the full death benefit when the person dies. The policy owner receives nothing more than the cash at trade-in.

    Viatical settlements are prohibited for life insurance policy owners in B.C., Alberta, Manitoba, Ontario, PEI, and Newfoundland and Labrador. They are permitted in Saskatchewan, New Brunswick, Nova Scotia, and Quebec.

2. Once a company that provides viatical settlements has acquired a policy, the policy is pooled with others to become an investment. Such investments have been described as a new asset class. They are more popular in the US which does not have regulatory provisions against such settlements and roughly ten times the population of Canada so many more come "on the market" than in this country.

Viatical or life settlements are available from Canadian companies (not insurance companies) as investments. As an investor in such a product, your invested capital is used to buy out the policies from the policy owners selling (some might say, sacrificing) their policies; your return is a function of when the life insured dies. If death occurs soon after the policy has been sold, few premiums will have been paid so the return will be higher than if death occurs at a later date and many premiums have been paid.

206: Why is health insurance so important?

The cost for medical care outside Canada can be financially ruinous. You just can't predict when an accident or sickness will occur and you should not risk that it won't happen to you or your spouse. This is true regardless of your age.

Most Canadians know, for instance, that snowbirds need health insurance when they spend their winters in the US. But, it is equally important, no matter how old you are, for a trip of any duration to the US or anywhere. You could have a heart attack looking at the price tags in a store on a Buffalo day-trip or a stroke on a weekend golf trip to Palm Springs. You could be hit by a bus in London or a taxi in Bangkok. You just don't know. Your medical bills could be tens of thousands of dollars a day. Can you afford to pay that out of pocket? If the answer is "no," then you know why health insurance is more than important --- it's essential.

207: How can I make sure my health insurance covers my costs?

There have been a lot of stories in the press about health insurance claims being denied by insurance companies. They report about people who have to pay the costs they incur outside Canada themselves despite the fact that they have health insurance. This seems particularly true when the claims are large.

Health insurance is essential when travelling outside Canada for a trip of any duration because provincial health care plans only pay a pittance for out-of-country claims.

To ensure a health policy will cover your claims, you must be entirely forthcoming about medical exams, conditions, sicknesses, and doctor or hospital visits or stays in the period of time during which pre-existing conditions are relevant to the policy. Answer every question on the application fully and honestly. Don't leave anything out: reveal all.

While it's true that "coming clean" could cause your premium to increase, the alternative of having to pay the bills yourself is not one you want to face.

Also, if you have an annual policy instead of insurance just to cover a single absence outside Canada, make sure you call the insurance company that issued the policy **before** every trip. Failing to notify the insurer of your intention to travel can, in itself, be a reason to deny your claim.

Also make note of the number of days' absence you are covered for in any one trip. If maximum coverage is 10 days, and you plan to be aware 12 days, you can "top-up" your coverage for the extra days. But, do not risk having no insurance for those days.

Some protection against claim denial may be provided by working with a life or health insurance agent directly when you apply for the policy instead of "going it alone" and completing an application yourself online or on the telephone. Good agents will make a lot of notes about your conversation in regards to your application in case they are called upon at a future date to support the information you provided.

208: I have heard "the biggest threat to your wealth is your health." What does that mean?

The cost of care as you age is expensive --- really expensive, and the costs are increasing. If that cost is being paid from your financial resources, those resources can be diminished or even exhausted by the expense. Plus, life spans are increasing. The expense of care may have to be paid for years, perhaps a decade or more. So, it is a simple equation: the cost multiplied by the length of time that cost is experienced can equal a very significant amount of cash. Your wealth can evaporate and the inheritances you planned to leave will no longer be possible because the money has been used to pay your living and care costs.

Not only are inheritances at risk, but what if the money runs out before you do? What happens then? If you cannot afford the care facility where you have been living, you will have to move to one within your financial reach.

How do you afford the care you need? This is where long-term care insurance comes in. It can pay care costs for as long as needed and ensure the estate is not depleted.

209: What does long-term care insurance cover?

Long-term care insurance (LTCI) will cover costs for you in a care facility or at home when your health has declined so that you have trouble with the so-called "activities of daily living," or you have cognitive impairment, such as memory loss. The activities of daily living include dressing, bathing, toileting, moving around, and eating. Once you need help, the LTCI will kick in to pay costs so that you may continue to live in your home with the assistance you need or the money may be paid towards facility care.

LTCI premiums can be quite steep so the younger you are when you apply, the better.

Using the insurance to pay your cost of continuing to live at home or to pay for living in a retirement or nursing home can save your estate hundreds of thousands of dollars.

210: Where do I buy long-term care insurance?

Life insurance companies sell long-term care insurance. The number of life insurance companies offering long-term care insurance is declining so your choice will be limited. There are fewer companies offering this form of insurance because long-term care insurance is a relatively new type of insurance and insurers initially did not charge enough for premiums. Therefore, some insurers found they could no longer afford to offer the insurance even though its need has never been greater than it will be in the near future.

211: What's the difference between critical illness insurance and long-term care insurance?

Critical illness insurance pays a lump sum when a person is diagnosed with one of the health conditions covered by the policy, and remains alive for 30 days following the diagnosis. The health conditions are very precise and requirements must be exactly met.

Long-term care insurance makes a monthly payment towards expenses incurred when a person is no longer able to perform simple duties such as dressing themselves or has a diminished capacity in thinking or memory. The money may be paid to enable independent living or for a care facility.

212: What is an annuity?

An annuity is a contract between you (the investor) and an issuer providing the product. You invest a sum in the annuity and that sum is repaid to you (minus expenses charged by the insurer) over time plus interest. Typically, money is received monthly.

The person who receives the annuity payment is called the annuitant.

Annuities are available for a specified period of time, such as 20 years; they are called term certain annuities. They are available through life insurance companies and banks.

Annuities are also available that are lifelong; this form is only available through life insurance companies. Some life annuities will provide a payment to a beneficiary if the annuitant dies and the income paid to the annuitant is less than the capital that was initially invested.

One form of annuity, the joint and last survivor annuity, is designed to provide an annuity payment for a couple. It continues to be paid after the death of the first spouse to the second spouse. When the second spouse dies, the annuity ends.

213: What forms of annuities are available?

There are two basic forms of annuity: one is an annuity that pays you over a specified period of time, such as 20 years. It is called a term certain annuity. A term certain to age 90 is the type of annuity you must buy if you choose to transfer some or all of the value of your RRSP to an annuity when your RRSP matures. You will receive a guaranteed income until age 90.

The other form of annuity is a life annuity; it pays until you die. Some life annuities make payments to beneficiaries after you die.

The best life annuity rate (that is, income based on your investment) is provided for a life straight annuity because there are no guarantees or other frills.

Annuities are available on an immediate or deferred basis.

They are also available in a form called a joint and last survivor annuity that covers a couple: payments continue after the first spouse dies to the second spouse.

214: Is there a role for annuities as retirement income?

An annuity is a secure source of income. They are not restricted for use only as retirement income; they can

151

be used throughout life. However, there is a strong association between retirement and annuities because annuities create an income stream that can take the place of an employer paycheque.

An annuity is one of the options available to you when your RRSP matures (at the end of the calendar year when you turn 71). This means you can rollover some or all of your RRSP into an annuity and the tax deferral on the value of the RRSP will continue.

An annuity is also an option for someone who has an employer pension that is in the form of a defined contribution plan (DCP). The amount in the DCP must be transferred to a suitable pension option when the employee with such a plan retires. A term certain annuity that provides an income to age 90 is one such option.

An annuity can also be purchased at any time with a lump sum of money or by regular contributions. This could be very suitable for someone who receives an inheritance and wants to turn that inheritance into a regular income.

Annuities had fallen out of favour when other forms of investment appeared to pay better rates of return. Annuities, however, are guaranteed and many people have happily traded in the uncertainty of those other investments for the "sure thing" they get with an annuity. The somewhat lower return of the annuity is more than compensated by the peace of mind the annuity owner enjoys.

215: What is an annuity rate?

It is the amount you receive based on your investment, which is directly linked to interest rates. For instance, in 2013, if you invested $100,000 in a straight life annuity, you might expect about $500/month income.

216: How does an annuity work?

An annuity is simply based on:

- an investment, either as a lump sum or by regular contributions. This forms the principal.

- an annuity rate, which is basically the interest rate in effect at the time applied to the amount invested.

- the length of time the annuity will be paid.

The principal plus interest is repaid to the person named as the annuitant on a regular basis over the length of time specified.

217: How much does it cost to buy an annuity?

Any fees, in the form of commission to an agent or to the company issuing the annuity, are hidden within the cost of the annuity. There is no out-of-pocket cost to you. The commission paid to the sales rep is about 1% of your investment.

218: Are there any disadvantages to annuities?

The interest rate offered at the time of purchase is locked in so you would not be able to benefit if rates increase in the future.

Also, annuities are meant to pay out on a regular basis. If you need a lump sum of money, you may not be able to get it out of the annuity or if you do, you will pay penalties and possibly ongoing fees to do so.

219: Where can I buy an annuity?

You can buy a life and a term certain annuity from a life insurance company or a life insurance agent.

You can buy a registered term certain annuity from a bank. This type of annuity is for those who select an annuity as an RRSP maturity option. This annuity will be structured to make payments to age 90.

220: Are annuities still relevant with today's low interest rates?

There is a school of thought that has recently brought annuities to the forefront of retirement income planning because of the guaranteed income they provide, and the peace of mind such a guarantee brings. There is no danger of outliving your financial resources if you have a life annuity. Also, there is no need for ongoing management decisions: once you buy the annuity you can count on it to provide for you.

It is fair to conclude that annuities are highly relevant even with today's low interest rates.

154

LUCKY STRIKE

There are two basic circumstances in which you suddenly find yourself the recipient of a large sum of money: one, when you are an inheritor of someone's estate and two, if you are an owner of a business who sells your business. Sorry, lotteries don't count!: the likelihood of winning is too remote to consider seriously. If you were so lucky, the same strategy would apply to a lottery win as for an inheritance.

QUESTIONS

221. What should I do with an inheritance?
222. Do I have to share my inheritance with my spouse?
223. Will I have to pay tax on an inheritance?
224. How much tax will I have to pay on the sale of my business?

HERE ARE THE ANSWERS...

221: What should I do with an inheritance?

1. Pay off debts.

2. Take the pay-yourself-first approach with the balance: extract 10% of what remains after paying the bills and have fun or do whatever makes you happy with the money.

3. Invest the balance. This is a perfect opportunity to be realistic about your investing chops. If the sum of money is large, you need independent financial expertise. This does not mean your banker! Find a financial planning firm that is fee based; your money will be well spent in paying those fees for the advice you will receive. Initially the investment could be short term while you gather information. Make sure an annuity is one of the options you consider since you will have the money available in a lump sum for its purchase. Look at an insured annuity (explained in our insurance chapter) as a way to enjoy the money during your lifetime and also provide an inheritance to your children or whomever you wish.

222: Do I have to share my inheritance with my spouse?

You can choose to keep an inheritance to yourself. To do so, you must not commingle the inherited sum with your family finances (family being you and your spouse) or use it to pay any family expenses. In reality, that is rather difficult but if you think you are your spouse are going to split up, that could be strong motivation to keep the funds separate.

223: Will I have to pay tax on an inheritance?

The sum you receive as an inheritance will be received from the executor of the estate of the deceased. The executor will have ensured all taxes have been paid before releasing funds to you. Any gains in the value of the inheritance once it is in your hands will be taxable. For instance, if you received $100,000 as an inheritance, you would not pay tax on the money. However, if you invested it and earned $5,500 in dividends, the $5,500 would be declared on your taxes.

224: How much tax will I have to pay on the sale of my business?

The person who sells shares of a qualified Canadian small business is entitled to a $750,000 capital gains exemption. Any amount greater than that will be taxed as a capital gain.

You should seek tax expertise before selling to ensure that the sale is accomplished with the greatest tax efficiency.

INVESTMENTS

This information focusses on general investment concepts relevant to retirees; it is not an overview of specific investment products, their strengths and weaknesses. Suitability is a particular concern and it arises in many answers.

QUESTIONS

225. What are the best investments for me when I'm retired?
226. How much should I withdraw from my savings every year?
227. How can I create an income stream from my investment portfolio?
228. What is the safest investment?
229. When should I start making withdrawals from my investments after I retire?
230. How should I invest after I retire?
231. What kinds of investing fees should I be aware of?
232. Should I use online investing?
233. How do I know my investment advisor is right for me?
234. Are there any investments just for retirees?
235. Is my investment advisor overcharging me?
236. Who can I trust with my investments?

237. What protection do I have against losses in
      my investments?
238. What is important information to have about
      investing and investments as I retire?
239. Are mutual funds suitable for retirees?
240. What happens to my non-registered investment
      accounts when I die?
241. Is it appropriate at this stage of life to own stocks?
242. Are there any investing strategies I could use to try
      and better my returns?
243. How should I invest my RRIF?
244. Can a GIC be transferred in kind?
245. How can I get the best rate on investments such as
      GICs or annuities?
246. What should I know about annuities?
247. I've always wanted to play the stock market and
      now I have the time. How could I start?
248. How is a Canada Premium Bond different from a
      Canada Savings Bond?
249. Are there any investments I should avoid
      during retirement?

HERE ARE THE ANSWERS...

225: What are the best investments for me when I'm retired?

The best investments for you are investments that you understand completely, and feel 100% comfortable having. To achieve understanding and a high comfort level you should:

- Be able to describe exactly what the investment is, let's say as if you were explaining it to someone who was considering putting money into that investment;

- Know what fees are associated with the investment, including the fees to buy, ongoing fees, and when it's time to sell;

- Find out whether fees are negotiable and on what basis;

- Have a basic understanding of how the person who sold you the investment gets paid: commission? Salary? Both? You don't need to know dollar amounts but you should know the fundamental compensation structure.

- Understand how the investment grows and how the growth on that investment is taxed: will it be as income, dividends, or capital gains?

- Know when tax is applied against the investment, i.e., every year? When you sell? When you die?

- Understand any guarantees associated with the investment and the conditions for payment of those guarantees;

- Know how long the period of investment is: is it open-ended or does the investment mature at a certain time? Is it redeemable before its maturity date, and is there a penalty for redeeming early?

- Honestly assess your own tolerance for risk and compare it to the risk of the investment;

- Ensure that a maturity date of the investment aligns with your income needs. For instance, a 5-year GIC would be a poor choice if you can see you will need some of that money in three years.

- Deal only with a reputable firm. If working with an investment firm you should check with the Investment Industry Regulatory Organization of Canada (IIROC). The dealers they regulate can be found here: **http://www.iiroc.ca/industry/Pages/ Dealers-We-Regulate.aspx**

- Mutual fund firms can be checked with the Mutual Fund Dealers Association (MFDA) here: **http://www.mfda.ca/members/members.html**

- Insurance agents should be checked with the provincial insurance commission for the province you live in.

226: How much should I withdraw from my savings every year?

The safe withdrawal rate (SWR) describes the percentage of an investment portfolio that can be withdrawn annually without depleting the portfolio. In other words, whatever you withdraw is more or less replaced by the returns on investments that remain in the account and you will never run out of money.

The magic number for the safe withdrawal rate is the subject of a great deal of debate. It depends very much on the performance of the investments in the account. The most cautious number suggested as a SWR is 3%, 4% is typically used, and some suggest a rate as high as 6% if very stringent withdrawal rules are followed.

For more information, see: Withdrawal Rate Strategies for Creating Retirement Income from a Portfolio at: **http://moneyover55.about.com/od/howtoinvest/a/ goldengoose.htm** Note this is US information, not endorsed by the authors.

Therefore, using the SWR of 4%, you would withdraw $4,000 annually from a portfolio valued at $100,000.

Coincidentally, if you have a RRIF at age 65, the percentage you must withdraw that year to meet your minimum withdrawal requirement is ... 4%!

227: How can I create an income stream from my investment portfolio?

If your investment portfolio consists of stocks and/or mutual funds, you can take what is called a systematic withdrawal --- in other words a regular withdrawal---that can be calculated in one of four ways. You will sell as much of your investment as necessary to provide:

- a fixed-dollar amount, such as $500 a month, until the account is depleted;

- a dollar amount over a fixed period of time in which the time period dictates the amount received, such as an account worth $200,000 will be taken over 20 years so therefore $10,000 a year is received as income (in fact, the period of time would end up being somewhat longer due to the returns that the account would continue to generate after withdrawals began or the withdrawals could be slightly larger to take returns into account);

- a ratio of account value, such as 4%;

- a life expectancy-adjusted amount in which you assume your lifespan and divide that number of years into the account value.

Remember, that if your investments are in a registered account, you will not receive the tax advantages of capital gains or dividends. Your withdrawals will be taxed at the same rate as if interest was paid.

228: What is the safest investment?

The safest investments are those guaranteed by the Government of Canada. These include Canada Savings Bonds, Canada Premium Bonds, and Treasury Bills. For all intents and purposes, Guaranteed Investment Certificates and savings accounts or other investment products offered by Canadian banks are also entirely safe since the likelihood of one of the big banks failing is virtually inconceivable.

229: When should I start making withdrawals from my investments after I retire?

When you start withdrawals will be the result of when you need money, and if you have a RRIF or LIF. If your investments are held within a RRIF or LIF, you must make minimum withdrawals. RRIFs established before 1992 have a different withdrawal schedule than those set up since that date.

If your investments are held in a non-registered account, the choice is yours. Investment income is part of net income and will therefore be a factor in the income on which your OAS is based. When income is higher than $71,000 (2013) OAS will be reduced, and when income is higher than $115,000 (2013) OAS will be eliminated.

Please see the chapter on RRSPs and RRIFs for the schedule on minimum RRIF withdrawals, and see Income Tax for thoughts on what order to take withdrawals.

230: How should I invest after I retire?

There is one important factor to bear in mind when investing during retirement: it becomes very difficult to make up for losses. This is due to the fact that you probably make less money since you are no longer working and so you don't have as much money available to invest, and time is no longer on your side. You may not have the years you need to compensate for losses or to count on compounding to make up shortfalls.

In fact, for these reasons, Moshe Milevsky, an expert on retirement income who teaches at York University in Toronto, calls the five years before and after the date of retirement the retirement risk zone.

Therefore, investing during retirement should gravitate towards the safe, secure, and guaranteed forms of investment that are available.

Whatever type of investment you choose, you should always stick with your comfort level. This is known as the suitability principle in the investment business. If you are totally comfortable with high-tech start-ups, and you fully understand the consequences of losses associated with such investing, then go for it.

231: What kinds of investing fees should I be aware of?

All investments have fees to compensate the firm providing the investment and the person who sells them; some fees are more visible than others.

The fees that take money out of your pocket are probably of highest concern. These would include sales charges and management expense ratio (MER) charges for mutual funds, and commissions on equity purchases and sales.

Note that sales charges on mutual funds typically decline over time. This is just one reason that most mutual funds are not suitable for short-term investing. The MER does not decline; the charge is applied to your mutual fund every year you own units in the fund. The MER varies by the need for management: for instance, a money market fund needs very little management and so charges a very low MER. An equity fund requires a lot of management; its MER will be much higher than the MER for the money market fund.

The MER is charged to everyone invested in a mutual fund. It is always expressed as a percentage. It affects your net return as follows: Return on fund minus MER = net return (for instance: 7% - 2% = 5%)

232: Should I use online investing?

Online investing saves you money in fees. However, you will not get advice about your proposed or existing investment, and you will not develop a personal relationship with an advisor. You will have to determine whether the absence of advice and the relationship are worth the amount you save.

If you will be investing online, make certain that you have effective, highly secure passwords in place on your computer and for your account(s). Do not use public computers in which your financial information could be stored and retrieved by someone else.

233: How do I know my investment advisor is right for me?

First, you must determine that he or she is properly licensed to sell the products he or she represents. You will also want to ensure that your advisor agrees with your investing philosophy: if you aren't comfortable with risky investments, he or she must respect that and work within your comfort level. You should also make sure that he or she is professional and promptly returns your phone calls and attends meetings regularly and on time.

The best advisors check in with their clients on an ongoing basis, when things are going well and when they aren't. If you hear from yours just once a year, chances are you need another advisor.

234: Are there any investments just for retirees?

No. Retirees have access to the same range of investments as people of all ages.

Annuities are often associated with retirement because they provide a steady income and, in essence, become a retirement paycheque.

Some mutual funds are designed to provide greater exposure to equities in early years (in an effort to get higher returns) and then, over time, adjust towards less risky holdings in tandem with the increasing age of the investor. By the time of retirement, the fund will be invested in very low-risk products such as a mortgage fund or bond fund. This is intended to align risk (and returns) with risk tolerance, which is known to decline with age.

Guaranteed Minimum Withdrawal Benefit Plans and Guaranteed Lifetime Withdrawal Benefit Plans meet the needs of retirees due to the steady income stream they provide. Please see the insurance chapter for details on these plans.

235: Is my investment advisor overcharging me?

It appears to the investing public that there are two types of fee arrangements for investment accounts: fee-for-service and no fee. In fact, no-fee firms do charge fees, but those fees are hidden in the cost of the investments they sell.

Fee-for-service firms charge an amount annually to manage your account. This fee is on top of other fees they earn through the products they sell, such as the commission they receive by selling stocks and bonds. The benefit of such an arrangement is the attention you will receive, coupled with analysis of your needs, with recommendations based on those needs. There should be less pressure on you.

No-fee firms and advisors are compensated by the products and services you buy and sell with them, or by salary when they are part of a large organization, such as a bank, that wants to keep you in house for all your financial business. The benefit of working with such firms and individuals is that you don't pay an annual fee. However, you won't receive much attention unless your account is sufficiently large to warrant a return on their time spent.

236: Who can I trust with my investments?

It is of paramount importance to first check that your proposed or existing advisor is properly licensed. The number of reps who are caught practicing without a license is shocking. Never assume a person is licensed because they appear to be genuine. Don't trust your family or friends' opinions about who they work with since they may not have done their due diligence.

Do your homework for your own protection. Check licensing as follows:

- mutual fund sales representatives through the Mutual Fund Dealer's Association (MFDA);

- stockbrokers through the Investment Industry Regulatory
Organization of Canada (IIROC);

- life insurance agents through the insurance regulator of each province (check your government listings for your province).

After you establish that the proper licensing is in place, who you trust should be the result of:

- the professionalism of the advisor as shown by his or manner towards you in meetings, phone conversations, and other communications;

- whether the advisor seems to respect issues of privacy and confidentiality;

- who the advisor works for and with;

- whether his or her recommendations seem tailored to your needs and circumstances;

- whether he or she has any interest in getting to know you and understand your concerns;

- your gut feeling about whether this is someone who seems to have your best interests at heart.

It is entirely appropriate to interview prospects for the position to find one you like and trust. After all, it's your money you are handing over.

237: What protection do I have against losses in my investments?

If you have a guaranteed investment, then you will be protected against market losses. Guaranteed investments include:

- Guaranteed Investment Certificates;

- Annuities;

- Segregated funds;

- Savings accounts at financial institutions;

- Canada Savings Bonds;

- Canada Premium Bonds;

- Treasury Bills (Canadian);

- Some bonds, such as those issued by the Government of Canada and the provinces.

You are also protected against losses to specified limits if the firm holding your accounts becomes insolvent.

- Investment Industry Regulatory Organization of Canada (IIROC) firms are insured by the Canadian Investor Protection Fund (CIPF).

- Mutual Fund Dealer's Association (MFDA) firms are insured by the Investor Protection Corporation (IPC).

- Insurance companies are insured by Assuris.

- Banks and similar financial institutions are covered by the Canada Deposit Insurance Corporation (CDIC).

However, losses in the value of non-guaranteed investments due to market conditions are not covered.

238: What is important information to have about investing and investments as I retire?

Past performance is no guarantee of future results.

239: Are mutual funds suitable for retirees?

Mutual fund investing is designed for the long term, so if you are a young retiree who anticipates living to a great old age, they may be right. You will not want to find yourself in a position that you must redeem part of your mutual fund investment before its sales charge has been eliminated.

There are many, many types of mutual funds so it is essential you understand the risk of the fund before you commit to investing. Before investing, you will be provided with information about the fund, its investing strategy, and its fees. Read this information carefully. Never assume future returns will be equal to, greater than, or less than what has come before.

Also remember that if your mutual funds are in a registered account, like a RRIF, you will be taxed on withdrawals at the same rate as income or interest. You do not receive the benefit of the capital gains tax or dividend tax rate.

240: What happens to my non-registered investment accounts when I die?

Your accounts may name a beneficiary:

- if the beneficiary is your spouse, the accounts will become the property of the spouse.

- if the beneficiary is not your spouse, the investments can be sold or there can be a deemed disposition of the investments at the time of your death. In this case, the investments are not sold but they are treated as if they were sold to determine how much tax must be paid by the inheritor(s) to retain those investments. Your estate pays the tax.

If you own the account as a joint tenancy account with rights of survivorship (JTWROS) – with one of your children for instance -- the account can rollover to the other joint owner without probate tax providing the account is not structured as a JTWROS simply to avoid probate fees.

241: Is it appropriate at this stage of life to own stocks?

There is no reason not to own stocks per se when retired providing you are comfortable with the concept of losing money. If you are confident that day-to-day losses won't keep you awake at night because over time the stock market has been shown to gain in value, then stocks might be a good choice.

Also, consider that some stocks pay dividends. If you take those dividends as cash, instead of reinvesting them, you can create income. Dividends from qualified Canadian companies are taxed at a lower rate than interest. They must be held in a non-registered investment account (not your RRSP or RRIF) for you to receive the better tax rate.

242: Are there any investing strategies I could use to try and better my returns?

Laddering is a strategy that can help you to avoid interest rate risk. That risk is experienced when an investment, such as a GIC, matures and the interest rate for renewal is lower than what the GIC had been earning. If multiple investments mature simultaneously, the risk of earning lower interest across the board is compounded.

Laddering sees investments in products with specified terms such as GICs or bonds mature at different dates. The hope is that an average higher rate of return will be obtained.

Some retirement income planners stress the need for equities (stocks and bonds) in the portfolio of retirees because of the probability of higher returns. This strategy carries significant risk in that there is no certainty equities will produce higher returns in the time frame you have available. However, again, this is a personal choice based on your risk tolerance.

243: How should I invest my RRIF?

You can continue the investments in your RRIF that you had in your RRSP; all the same investments are available in both accounts and when the time comes to mature the RRSP to a RRIF the investments simply rollover from one account to the other. They do not have to be sold and then repurchased from money in the RRIF.

Typically, investments during retirement lean more towards those that are low risk or guaranteed since the ability to recoup investment losses is hampered by a lack of earnings. However, the choice is entirely personal as to what you invest in.

However you invest, you will receive the proceeds (both the return of your capital and any growth on that capital) from your RRIF as interest for income tax purposes. Therefore, there is no tax advantage to choosing one form of investment over another; the advantage lies in the hoped-for better returns.

244: Can a GIC be transferred in kind?

A GIC can only be transferred out of your RRIF to another account if it is specified as being transferable and assignable.

245: How can I get the best rate on investments such as GICs or annuities?

Shop around. There are differences between providers and there is no need to show loyalty to one provider over another.

The more money you have to invest will often see better rates offered so you may need to consolidate some accounts to benefit from this approach.

It is also known that working through a broker will bring a better rate than if you are a general investor. The Registered Deposit Brokers Association (www.rdba.ca) can help you find a broker in your neighbourhood.

246: What should I know about annuities?

Annuities pay back the investment you make in them over a period of time or for life. That payment amount is linked to interest rates so in today's low interest rate environment their payment rate is lower than when interest rates are higher.

The interest rate on your annuity is set when you buy the annuity; the money you receive as your annuity payment will not increase or decrease unless you have a variable annuity.

Annuities are an excellent product to ensure retirement savings are parceled out and not depleted by spending sprees. However, they do not provide flexibility. If unexpected expenses come up, you can't get more from the annuity than you are already receiving.

It can also be very difficult to extract yourself from an annuity. There will be fees and penalties if the insurer even permits termination of the contract.

247: I've always wanted to play the stock market and now I have the time. How could I start?

Since you now have the time, you could develop stock market investing as a hobby providing:

- you spend the money to learn about the risks of stock market investing from a reputable source such as ShareOwner Education at **http://www.shareowner.com;**

- you set aside a small amount of money (an amount you can afford to lose) and use that as your seed capital. If you make money buying and selling stocks, your funds available for investing will grow from that initial amount of capital. If you lose money, your losses are limited to that capital and your retirement has not been jeopardized.

248: How is a Canada Premium Bond different from a Canada Savings Bond?

Canada Savings Bonds are now only available through payroll deduction. For this reason alone, they may be unavailable to you if you no longer work or you work where they are not offered in a payroll plan.

Like a Canada Savings Bond, the Canada Premium Bond (CPB) is a guaranteed investment offered by the

Government of Canada. It offers slightly better interest rates than a Canada Savings Bond because it is redeemed only on maturity and up to 30 days after. CPBs have a three-year term-to-maturity and a set interest rate for the term. They are available through investment dealers, financial institutions, and directly from Canada Savings Bond Customer Service. Here is contact info: **http://www.csb.gc.ca/contact-us/certificated-bond-owners**

249: Are there any investments I should avoid during retirement?

You should not invest in any product in which you do not fully understand and, similarly, understand how you get a return on the investment. Know, too, if the money will be tied up for a period of time and if so, how long, how you get your money out, and how much it would cost to get your money out. Ensure you are comfortable with the risk of each investment.

INCOME TAX

Tax reduction strategies have also been discussed in the other chapters; these questions will help to fill in some of the remaining gaps on this important subject.

QUESTIONS

250. Should I have a TFSA if I'm retired?
251. What is the point of income splitting?
252. Are withdrawals from the TFSA considered part of the income on which my OAS is based?
253. What strategies can I use to pay less tax?
254. How do I split income with my spouse?
255. What is not eligible income for splitting?
256. How much money can I save by income splitting?
257. Should I use a spousal RRSP to split income?
258. Who pays tax on the withdrawals from a spousal plan?
259. Is there a best way to receive income from a tax perspective?
260. Is there any way to transfer wealth to my family after my death tax free?

HERE ARE THE ANSWERS...

250: Should I have a TFSA if I'm retired?

A TFSA can be very useful to hold funds that had to be withdrawn from a RRIF due to the annual minimum withdrawal requirement, but that are not needed for short-term living expenses. The money withdrawn from the RRIF will be taxable but then once in the TFSA it becomes tax-free.

If the money was instead moved into an investment account, then any returns in that account would be taxed. This would be double taxation.

251: What is the point of income splitting?

The point of splitting income between spouses is to redistribute income between two spouses who have different marginal tax rates.

Let's say you and your spouse have different tax rates, and your rate is the higher of the two. Moving income from you to your spouse can decrease your taxes. Your spouse pays income tax on the money according to his or her lower rate. For the strategy to work, the amount of money transferred to your spouse must not be an amount that would move him or her to a higher tax bracket or the tax advantage may be lost.

252: Are withdrawals from the TFSA considered part of the income on which my OAS is based?

No.

253: What strategies can I use to pay less tax?

The Canadian tax system is pretty much based on the idea that if you earn money, you do your bit for the country and pay tax on that money. Many ways to pay less tax call on you to earn less. For many people earning less is not an option. And, quite frankly, it doesn't make sense to earn less money just to lower your tax bill.

One legitimate means at your disposal is to base your RRIF withdrawals on the age of your spouse, if he or she is younger than you. This means a lower amount will have to be taken as a minimum and you will have less taxable income.

Another way to reduce taxes is to split income. Splitting income is possible with RRIF withdrawals and annuity and pension income. It only makes sense if you and your spouse are in different tax brackets. The income is split so that the one who pays tax at a higher rate has less income, and the other who pays tax at a lower rate has more income.

Making use of the senior's pension income credit reduces taxes by up to $150 per person. The credit applies to the first $2,000 of pension, RRIF or annuity income (neither Canada Pension Plan nor Old Age Security payments qualify). It is claimed on the tax return.

Trusts are also an option but beyond the reach of many due to the expense of creating the trust and maintaining it. We feel a discussion of trusts is not appropriate in this volume.

254: How do I split income with my spouse?

You must both agree to the split and make what CRA calls a "joint election." You will attach CRA Form T1032 Joint Election to Split Income to both you and your spouse's income tax return and the information on both copies of the form must be the same.

You only split one income of the two you and your spouse both receive.

255: What is not eligible income for splitting?

You cannot split income received from:

- OAS;
- CPP/QPP;
- Income from a U.S. IRA;
- Foreign source pension income that is tax-free in Canada;
- Money received from a retirement compensation arrangement;
- Money from a RRIF that is transferred to an RRSP, another RRIF, or annuity.

256: How much money can I save by income splitting?

The Royal Bank of Canada reports in its newsletter, The Navigator, that you will save $6,000 to $9,000 per year if you and your spouse both have taxable income of $50,000 instead of you alone having income of $100,000.

They also say that you can save up to 14% in federal tax (depending on your personal circumstances) and save on provincial tax by splitting income.

You can also benefit by splitting income to lower your taxable income and therefore, by keeping your income lower, you will not lose as much or all of your OAS payment.

257: Should I use a spousal RRSP to split income?

Yes, providing your spouse is in a lower tax bracket.

You can contribute to a spousal plan after you are 71 if your spouse is still able to accept contributions to his or her plan and you have unused contribution room or earned income.

258: Who pays tax on the withdrawals from a spousal plan?

If you make a spousal contribution this year, and your husband or wife withdraws the money this year or in the next two years, you will pay tax on the withdrawal.

This is also true of spousal RRIF withdrawals above the minimum withdrawal amount. So, if you made a contribution to a spousal plan when your spouse was 71, and the plan was matured to a RRIF at the end of that year, you would be taxed on any withdrawal above the minimum for the next two years.

This does not apply if you and your spouse are living apart due to marriage breakdown, if you or your spouse becomes a non-resident of Canada, or if the RRSP is used to buy an annuity.

259: Is there a best way to receive income from a tax perspective?

If you are earning less income than you will in the future – because, for instance, your pension plan payments haven't started yet – it may be best to withdraw more than the minimums required from your RRIF or locked-in accounts. The money you receive will be taxed at your marginal tax rate in effect at the time, which should be lower because your income is lower.

Leave your tax-preferred income, such as dividend income or capital gains, to the time when you are in a higher tax bracket because your pension income has started.

Also, since TFSA withdrawals do not contribute to income on which your OAS is based, it could make sense to withdraw from your TFSA after you take your minimums from other plans.

260: Is there any way to transfer wealth to my family after my death tax free?

A life insurance death benefit is tax-free when it is paid to a beneficiary that is not your estate. You pay the premiums and your beneficiary benefits from the policy proceeds. When the proceeds are directed to your estate, they may be subject to probate fees according to the province in which you live.

IS THAT ALL THERE IS TO LEARN?

We guess this makes 261 questions in the book! But, let's not make light of the questions we've tackled and the importance of the subject of retirement.

When you begin to plan your retirement income or begin retirement itself you don't have the benefit of experience: it's a trial-and-error business. Luckily, few things are carved in stone so as you learn, and learn what is best for you, changes are not only possible but probable.

Learning is key. It opens the doors to new possibilities and keeps you on top of new developments. It seems that every year regulations change, and some of those changes can have a very significant impact on your finances. One of the best and easiest ways to keep up with changes in government pensions is to visit the Service Canada website periodically.

Take charge of what you need to know, err on the side of caution when it comes to decisions, and do what is right for you. Always be prepared to challenge advice you are given and regardless of how you plan, or who you plan with, ask questions and get answers you can understand. Seek right answers; live a happy and wise retirement!